Come and See

Catholic Bible Study

Acts and Letters

(Acts, Romans, 1 and 2 Corinthians, Galatians, Ephesians, Philippians, Colossians, 1 and 2 Thessalonians, Philemon)

by

Father Joseph L. Ponessa, S.S.D.

and

Laurie Watson Manhardt, Ph.D.

Emmaus Road Publishing
827 North Fourth Street
Steubenville, OH 43952

All rights reserved. Published in 2008
Printed in the United States of America

Library of Congress Control Number: 2008928600
ISBN: 978-1-931018-51-7

Cover design and layout by
Jacinta Calcut, Image Graphics and Design www.image–gd.com

Cover artwork:
Melissa Dayton, The Descent of the Holy Spirit
www.pearlsofgracefineart.com

Nihil obstat: Reverend Monsignor Joseph N Rosie, STL, *Censor Librorum*
Imprimatur: Most Reverend John M. Smith, Bishop of Trenton
April 24, 2008

The *nihil obstat* and *imprimatur* are official declarations
that a book is free of doctrinal or moral error.

For additional information on the "Come and See ~ Catholic Bible Study"
series visit www.CatholicBibleStudy.net

COME AND SEE

Catholic Bible Study

Acts and Letters

(Acts, Romans, 1 and 2 Corinthians, Galatians,
Ephesians, Philippians, Colossians,
1 and 2 Thessalonians, Philemon)

Introduction

At the name of Jesus every knee should bow, in heaven and on earth and under the earth, and every tongue confess that Jesus Christ is Lord, to the glory of the Father.
Philippians 2:10–11

People have been writing letters to each other for thousands of years. The great and the lowly, the rich and the poor, in every language and every nation, have communicated over great distances by means of the written word. They have shared information, described historical events, poured out their thoughts and revealed their feelings. Classical authors, like Seneca, wrote epistles of a literary nature, intended for a wide readership. Since the earliest days, the Popes in Rome have sent encyclical letters to the bishops of the world to promote harmony and to propel the teaching Magisterium of the church.

Letters become more frequent in the pages of the Bible as literacy spreads and the scribe becomes more prominent in society. The Old Testament contains letters of introduction (2 Kings 5:6), letters of invitation (1 Chronicles 30:1), letters of accusation (Daniel 4:7) and letters of appointment (Ezra 7:11). The prophet Jeremiah writes to the exiles in Babylon ("Letter of Jeremiah" or Baruch 6) and they write back (Baruch 1—2). The twenty-seven books of the New Testament include twenty-one letters written by five apostles—Peter, James, John, Jude, and Paul.

Paul of Tarsus is one of the most influential letter-writers of all time. Paul began sending letters before any of the four gospels were put on paper. His First Letter to the Thessalonians is commonly accepted as the first piece of writing in the New Testament, probably in the early 50s AD. By means of his letters, Paul maintained an apostolic presence over a large swath of the Roman world, so that his role in the spread of Christianity can hardly be overemphasized.

The thirteen surviving Pauline letters fall into two groups. About the year 50, during the course of his missionary journeys, Paul wrote correctional and disciplinary letters back to communities that he had recently visited. Paul left Thessalonika and went to Corinth, from where he wrote letters back to the Thessalonians. Then Paul left Corinth and went to Ephesus, and from there he wrote letters back to the Corinthians. These letters present advanced lessons in Christianity to those who have already started on the way, and have begun to stumble.

Later in the same decade, Paul found himself imprisoned for several years in Caesarea, the Roman military capital of the Holy Land. A second wave of letters ensued, not letters of discipline this time but letters of teaching. At first he wrote back to communities he had already visited—Philippi, Ephesos, Colossae—but then he wrote his greatest work, the letter to the community of Rome, which he had not yet visited. These later letters become more systematic in their exposition of Christian doctrine, and in a way more fundamental. For all Paul knew, each letter he wrote from prison would be his last, and he tried to pour the fullness of his faith into each of them. From the valley of the shadow of death, he sent out inspired teachings to the whole world, and to all time.

One of Paul's companions, who was there when he wrote the imprisonment letters, was the physician Luke, who later wrote the story of the early church, entitled Acts of the Apostles. The human authors Paul and Luke set forth the foundation of the church's teachings about the great issues of redemption, faith, grace, virtue, and much, much more. The Holy Spirit has something in store for each of us in the great teachings of the Apostle to the Nations and of his disciple the evangelist Luke. We will never know what blessings await us until we launch into these writings and look for the pearl of great price that they contain.

What You Need

To do this Bible Study, you will need a Catholic Bible, and a *Catechism of the Catholic Church* (CCC). When choosing a Bible, remember that the Catholic Bible contains seventy-three books. If you find Sirach in your Bible's table of contents, you have a complete Catholic Bible. The Council of Hippo approved these seventy-three books in AD 393, and this has remained the official canon of Sacred Scripture since the Fourth Century. The Council of Trent in AD 1545 authoritatively reaffirmed these divinely inspired books for inclusion in the canon of the Bible. The Douay-Rheims, one of the first English translations of the Catholic Bible, was completed in AD 1609.

For bible study purposes, choose a word-for-word, literal translation rather than a paraphrase. Some excellent translations are the Revised Standard Version Catholic Edition (RSVCE), the Jerusalem Bible (JB), and the New American Bible (NAB).

How To Do This Bible Study

1. Pray to the Holy Spirit to enlighten your mind and spirit.
2. Read the bible passages for the first chapter.
3. Read the commentary in this book.
4. Use your Bible and Catechism to write answers to the home study questions.
5. Find a small group and share your answers aloud on those questions.
6. Watch the videotape lecture that goes with this study.
7. End with a short wrap-up lecture and/or prayer.

Invite and Welcome Priests and Religious

Ask for the blessing of your pastor before you begin. Invite your pastor, associate pastor, deacon, visiting priests, and religious sisters to participate in bible study. Invite priests and religious to come and pray with the bible study members, periodically answer questions from the question box, or give a wrap-up lecture. Accept whatever they can offer to the bible study. However, don't expect or demand anything from them. Appreciate that the clergy are very busy and don't add additional burdens. Accept with gratitude whatever is offered.

Practical Considerations

- ✓ Ask God for wisdom about whom to study with, where, and when to meet. Gather a small prayer group to pray for your bible study and your specific needs. Pray to discern God's will in your particular situation.
- ✓ Show this book to your pastor and ask for his approval and direction.
- ✓ Choose a day of the week and time to meet.
- ✓ Invite neighbors and friends to a "Get Acquainted Coffee" to find out who will make a commitment to meet for 60 to 90 minutes each week for bible study.
- ✓ Find an appropriate location. Start in someone's home or in the parish hall if the space is available and the pastor will allow it.
- ✓ Hire a babysitter for mothers with young children and share the cost amongst everyone, or find some volunteers to provide childcare.
- ✓ Consider a cooperative arrangement, in which women take turns caring for the children. All women, even grandmothers and women without children, should take turns, serving the children as an offering to God.

Pray that God will anoint specific people to lead your study. Faithful, practicing Catholics are needed to fill the following positions:

- ✓ **Teachers** – take responsibility to read commentaries and prepare a fifteen to twenty minute wrap-up lecture after the small group discussion and video.
- ✓ **Song Leaders** – lead everyone in singing a short hymn to begin bible study.
- ✓ **Prayer Leaders** – open bible study with a short prayer.
- ✓ **Children's Teachers** – teach the young children who come to bible study.
- ✓ **Coordinators** – communicate with parish personnel about needs for rooms, microphones, and video equipment. Make sure rooms are left in good shape.
- ✓ **Small Group Facilitators** will be needed for each small group. Try to enlist two mature Catholics who are good listeners to serve together as co-leaders for each small group and share the following responsibilities:

    - ✓ Pray for each member of your small group every day.
    - ✓ Make a nametag for each member of the group.
    - ✓ Meet before the study to pray with other leaders.
    - ✓ Discuss all the questions in the lesson each week.
    - ✓ Begin and end on time.
    - ✓ Make sure that each person in the group shares each week. Ask each person to read a question and have the first chance to answer it.
    - ✓ In the discussion group you may go around in a circle, so that each person can

look forward to his or her turn to read a question. After reading the question, the reader can answer the question or pass, and then others can feel free to add additional comments.

✓ Make sure that no one person dominates the discussion, including you!

✓ Keep the discussion positive and focused on the week's lesson.

✓ Speak kindly and charitably. Steer the conversation away from any negative or uncharitable speech, complaining, arguing, gossip, or griping. Don't badmouth anyone or any church.

✓ Listen well! Keep your ears open and your eyes on the person speaking.

✓ Give your full attention to the one speaking. Be comfortable with silence. Be patient. Encourage quieter people to share first. Ask questions.

✓ If questions, misunderstandings, or disagreements arise, refer them to the question box for a teacher to research or the parish priest to answer later.

✓ Arrange for a social activity each month.

More Practical Considerations

✓ Jesus chose a group of twelve apostles. So, perhaps twelve or thirteen people make the best small groups. When you get too many, break into two groups.

✓ A group of teenagers or a young adult group could be facilitated by the parish priest or a young adult leader.

✓ Men share best with men and women with women. If you have a mixed bible study, organize separate men's groups led by men and women's groups led by women. In mixed groups, some people tend to remain silent.

✓ Offer a married couples' group, if two married couples are willing to lead the group. Each person should have his or her own book.

✓ Sit next to the most talkative person in the group and across from the quietest. Use eye contact to affirm and encourage quieter people to speak up. Serve everyone and hear from everyone.

✓ Listening in bible study is just as important as talking. Evaluate each week. Did everyone share? Am I a good listener? Did I really hear what others shared? Was I attentive or distracted? Did I affirm others? Did I talk too much?

✓ Share the overall goal aloud with all of the members of the group. We want to hear from each person in the group, sharing aloud each time the group meets.

✓ Make sure that people share answers only on those questions on which they have written answers. Don't just share off the top of your head. Really study.

✓ Consider a nursing mothers' group in which mothers can bring their infants and hold them while sharing their home study questions.

✓ Family groups can work together on a family bible study night, reading the commentary and scriptures aloud and helping one another to find answers in the Bible and Catechism.

✓ Parents or older siblings can read to young children and help the youngsters to do the crafts in the children's bible study book.

Social Activities

God has created us as social creatures, needing to relate communally. Large parishes make it difficult for people to get to know one another. Some people can belong to a parish for years without getting to know others. Newcomers may never get noticed and welcomed. Bible study offers an opportunity for spiritual nourishment as well as inclusion and hospitality. Occasional social activities are recommended in this book. These socials are simple, fun, and easy. In planning your social activities be a good sport and try to attend with your group.

✓ Agree on a time when most of the group can meet. This could be right before or after bible study or a different day of the week, perhaps even Saturday morning.
✓ Invite people to come to your home for the social time. Jesus was comfortable visiting the homes of the rich and the poor. So, whatever your circumstances, as a Christian you can offer hospitality to those God sends along your way.

"Do not neglect to show hospitality to strangers,
for thereby some have entertained angels unawares."
(Hebrews 13:2)

✓ Keep it simple! Just a beverage and cookies work well. Simplicity blesses others. People can squeeze together on a sofa or stand around the kitchen. Don't fuss.
✓ Help the group leader. If bible study meets in someone's home, invite the group to come to your place for the social time. Don't make the group leader do it all.
✓ If bible study meets at church, don't have all of the socials at church as well. Try to have some fellowship times in people's homes. Perhaps over the Christmas break you can go to someone's home for coffee and cookies after Christmas and before bible study starts up again.

Suggested Times for Socials

9:30–10:30 a.m. Saturday coffee   12:00–1:00 p.m. Luncheon

3:00–4:00 p.m.   Afternoon tea   8:00–9:00 p.m. Dessert

Modify times to meet your specific needs. If your parish has Saturday morning Mass at 9:00 a.m., adjust the time of your social to accommodate those members of the group who would like to attend Mass and need some time to get to the social. If lunch after bible study makes too long of a day for children who need naps, plan the social for a different day. A mother's group might meet after school when high school students are available to baby-sit.

Class Schedule

Accept responsibility for being a good steward of time. God gives each of us twenty-four hours every day. If bible study starts or ends late, busy people may drop out. Late starts punish the prompt and encourage tardiness. Be a good steward of time. Begin and end bible study with prayer at the agreed upon time. If people consistently arrive late or leave early, investigate whether you have chosen the best time for most people. You may have a conflict with the school bus schedule or the parish Mass schedule. Perhaps beginning a few minutes earlier or later could be a service to those mothers who need to pick up children from school, or those who attend daily Mass.

Possible Bible Study Class Schedules

Morning Class

9:30 a.m.	Welcome, song, prayer
9:40 a.m.	Video
9:55 a.m.	Small group discussion
10:40 a.m.	Wrap-up lecture and prayer

Afternoon Class

1:00 p.m.	Welcome, song, prayer
1:10 p.m.	Small group discussion
1:55 p.m.	Video
2:10 p.m.	Wrap-up lecture and prayer

Evening Class

7:30 p.m.	Welcome, song, prayer
7:40 p.m.	Video
8:00 p.m.	Small group discussion
8:40 p.m.	Wrap-up lecture and prayer

As you can see, the video could be shown either before or after the small group discussion, and either before, after, or instead of a wrap-up lecture. Whether or not you choose to use the videotapes, please begin and end with prayer.

Wrap-Up Lecture

Father Ponessa provides additional information in videotaped lectures, which are available for this study and can be obtained from Emmaus Road Publishing Company, 827 North Fourth Street, Steubenville, Ohio, 43952. You can obtain DVDs or videocassettes of these lectures by going to www.emmausroad.org on the Internet or by calling 1-800-398-5470. Videotaped lectures may be used in addition to, or in place of a wrap-up lecture, depending on your needs.

When offering a closing lecture, the presenter should spend extra time in prayer and study to prepare a good, sound lecture. The lecturer should consult several Catholic bible study commentaries and prepare a cohesive, orthodox lecture. Several members of the leaders' team could take turns giving wrap-up lectures. Also, invite priests, deacons, and religious sisters to give an occasional lecture.

The lecturer should:
- ✓ Be a faithful, practicing Catholic. Seek spiritual direction. Frequent the sacraments, especially the Eucharist and Reconciliation.
- ✓ Obtain the approval and blessing of your parish priest to teach.
- ✓ Use several different presenters whenever possible.
- ✓ Pray daily for all of the leaders and members of the study.
- ✓ Pray over the lesson to be studied and presented.

- ✓ Outline the bible passages to be studied.
- ✓ Identify the main idea of the bible study lesson.
- ✓ Find a personal application from the lesson. How can one make a practical response to God's word?
- ✓ Plan a wrap-up lecture with a beginning, a middle, and an end.
- ✓ Use index cards to keep focused. Don't read your lecture; talk to people.

- ✓ Proclaim, teach, and reiterate the teachings of the Catholic Church. Learn what the Catholic Church teaches, and proclaim the fullness of truth.
- ✓ Illustrate the main idea presented in the passage by using true stories from the lives of the saints, or the lives of contemporary Christians.
- ✓ Use visuals—a flip chart or overhead transparencies if possible.
- ✓ Plan a skit, act out a bible story, and interact with the group.

- ✓ Try to make the scriptures come alive for the people in your group.
- ✓ Provide a question box. Find answers to difficult questions or ask a parish priest to come and answer questions on occasion.
- ✓ When difficult or complex personal problems arise or are shared in the group, seek out the counsel of a priest.
- ✓ Begin and end on time. When you get to the end of your talk, stop and pray.

Challenges

"All scripture is inspired by God and profitable for teaching, for reproof, for correction, and for training in righteousness, that the man of God may be complete, equipped for every good work" (2 Timothy 3:16–17).

As Christians, all of us are weak and need God's mercy and forgiveness. Lay groups can attract people with problems and challenges. Don't try to be all things for all people. Jesus is the Savior, and we are only His servants. When problems loom, direct them to a priest or counselor. Bible study demands faithfulness to the task at hand, while praying for others in their needs. Saint Paul encourages us to "speak the truth in love . . . and be kind to one another, tenderhearted, forgiving one another, as God in Christ forgave you" (Ephesians 4:15, 32). Bible study provides the opportunity for us to search God's word for direction in our personal lives and to pray for, encourage, and sometimes gently admonish one another.

Memory requires more than a merely external registering of events. We can only receive and hold fast to the uttered word if we are involved inwardly. If something does not touch me, it will not penetrate; it will dissolve in the flux of memories and lose its particular face.

Above all it is a fact that understanding and preserving what is understood go together. If I have not really understood a thing, I will not be able to communicate it properly. Only by understanding do I receive reality at all; and understanding, in turn, depends on a certain measure of inner identification with what is to be understood. It depends on love. I cannot really understand something for which I have no love whatsoever.

… what is required is a memory of the heart, in which I invest something of myself. Involvement and faithfulness are not opposites: they are interdependent.

Pope Benedict XVI (Cardinal Joseph Ratzinger), *Seek That Which Is Above* (San Francisco, CA: Ignatius Press, 1986), pp. 100–101

A Prayer to the Holy Spirit

O Holy Spirit, Beloved of my soul, I adore You,
enlighten, guide, strengthen and console me.
Tell me what I ought to say and do, and command me to do it.
I promise to be submissive in everything You will ask of me,
and to accept all that You permit to happen to me,
only show me what is Your will.

Chapter 1

Birth of the Church – AD 29
Acts of the Apostles 1–2

**And Peter said to them,
Repent, and be baptized every one of you in the name of Jesus Christ
for the forgiveness of your sins; and you shall receive the gift of the Holy Spirit.**
Acts 2:38

"**Y**ou shall be my witnesses" (Acts 1:8). Eleven Jews stood staring up into the sky one Thursday in May of the Year 29 AD. They had just received the biggest task of all time. Their rabbi, Jesus of Nazareth, just before He disappeared before their eyes and ascended to His heavenly throne, had told them: "You shall be my witnesses in Jerusalem and in all Judea and Samaria and to the end of the earth" (Acts1:8). This commission focuses on three challenges:

1) **Jerusalem** would be difficult enough, since their rabbi had been crucified there only 43 days before, but at least the work was near at hand. From their place atop the Mount of Olives they could look across the Kidron Valley and see the Holy City, and the temple mount. There, Jews and godfearers from all the nations gathered on the holy days and would provide an audience for the apostles' witness. All they had to do was walk down one mountain and up another to begin fulfilling the first part of the commission.

2) **Judea and Samaria** presented a bigger challenge, especially Samaria. Jews and Samaritans reviled one another, maintained different holy sites, and waylaid each other at pilgrimage time. Jesus asked these eleven Galilean Jews to build a bridge where none had ever been built before.

3) **The end of the earth**—witnessing to the whole world raised the challenge to a whole new level. How could eleven men change the world? Even more, at no stage in all of their history had Jews tried to convert people of other nations. The Mosaic covenant bonded one people to Almighty God, and other peoples had no obligation to take the Torah upon themselves. Some of the prophets had spoken of a universal witness of Israel to the nations, but never did those prophecies translate into missionary activity. Jesus had asked something entirely new of His disciples, that they by their actions should take His movement to all the nations.

"**All these with one accord devoted themselves to prayer, together with the women and Mary the mother of Jesus**" (Acts 1:14). Christians of later times look back upon the first decades of the church's life as a privileged time, when those who had sat at the Master's feet, had heard His teachings with their own ears, and seen His miracles, especially His Resurrection, were still alive to tell the story in their own words. While the apostles lived, the church needed no New Testament. The apostles were the living testament.

The Blessed Virgin Mary occupied a unique place in the life of the earliest church. She had known her Son ten times longer than the apostles had. Therefore, for the remainder of her life, she sat at a position of honor in their company. Apparently among those who interviewed the Virgin Mother was a young man by the name of Lucas, who wrote the Gospel of Luke and the Acts of the Apostles. His Gospel is the source for much of Mary's biographical information, and he mentions her prominently at the beginning of the Acts of the Apostles as well (Acts 1:14).

Interestingly, the union between Mary and the apostles is one of prayer. Faithful Jews prayed three times a day. In the morning, at noon, and in the evening, the apostles prayed with Mary at their side. At no time of day did they exclude her from their assembly. Luke portrays the acts of the apostles as inseparable from the acts of Mary. She had given them the Rabbi who had called them to apostleship. As Mary and the apostles began to disappear one–by–one, the need arose for a Christian Scripture to supplement the received Hebrew Scripture. The oral teaching of the apostles coalesced into twenty-one letters, four Gospels, the Acts of the Apostles, and a Book of Revelation.

The Acts of the Apostles records the first thirty years of the missionary activity of the apostolic church. The book ends abruptly, because, in fact, the book remains unfinished to the end of time. The eleven men charged with the original commission propelled a movement with such momentum that the force of it would continue unabated for millennia. No other eleven men—or eleven thousand men—have ever had a comparable effect on human history.

"Peter stood up among the brethren" (Acts 1:15). Peter exercises the leadership role over the whole church both before and after the descent of the Holy Spirit. He could have said, "There is no rush. We can wait until after the Spirit comes, and then select someone to replace Judas. Then, with the help of the Spirit, we can do a better job of selection." Instead, he took a forthright action to ensure that a twelfth apostle would have a seat at the table to receive the Spirit along with the rest. Peter shows us all that the natural gifts do not have to wait for the supernatural gifts. Every gift carries with it the responsibility to be used, and delay is pointless.

After the outpouring of the Holy Spirit, Peter delivers the first sermon in the history of the church. He could have said, "John, you are the beloved, why don't you give a talk?" Or, "Matthew, you have the skills of a scribe, why don't you read a transcript of one of Jesus' talks, maybe the Sermon on the Mount?" But, Peter stands with authority before the crowd to deliver a magisterial address, and take charge of the development of doctrine in the church. The Christian movement is not some headless amoeba charging blindly into the future—the descent of the Holy Spirit does not preempt, but confirms the leadership of Peter and the apostles.

"When the day of Pentecost had come" (Acts 2:1). On the fiftieth day after Passover, the Jews celebrate the festival of Pentecost, one of the three high holydays requiring pilgrimage to the temple in Jerusalem. Jews in the Holy Land were close enough to

Jerusalem to attend all three festivals. Those in the diaspora, being spread over the world, could only come occasionally, but each Jewish community everywhere sent a delegation at least once a year. Those sent would deliver the temple tax to Jerusalem and bring back news of interest to the local community.

Of the three pilgrimage festivals, Pentecost drew the biggest crowds, because traveling conditions were best at that time of year. People could celebrate Passover with their own families and then have fifty days of travel time including the month of May to get to Jerusalem. Later, the Acts of the Apostles describe how Paul followed this pattern when he celebrated Passover with the community of Philippi and then hastened to Jerusalem in time for Pentecost, in order to deliver to the apostles the contributions of the Macedonian church (Acts 20–21).

Like Paul, the Jewish delegates reported first to a group of their own countrymen residing in Jerusalem, and that group accompanied them to the temple to consign the tax to the temple treasury. Every nation of the world had at least one synagogue in Jerusalem, where Jews from that country who lived in Jerusalem could meet weekly and where pilgrims from that country could report at festival time. Ancient sources indicate that the number of synagogues in the city at that period ranged from 365 to 480.

"Now there were dwelling in Jerusalem Jews, devout men from every nation under heaven" (Acts 2:5). Luke itemizes many of the nations represented in Jerusalem on the first Pentecost—Mesopotamia, Judea, Cappadocia, Pontus, Asia, Phrygia, Pamphylia, Egypt, Libya, Rome, Crete, Arabia. Many of those names are unfamiliar today. The diaspora Jews resided principally in cities, and the list of the capital cities will sound more familiar—Babylon, Jerusalem, Pergamon, Alexandria, Cyrene, Rome. Babylon holds first place on the list, because the Jewish community there was very numerous, ever since the time of the exile, but also because the Tower of Babel had been there, and the Pentecost event stands counterpoised to the Babel event. If Babel was the problem, Pentecost was the solution. At Babel, the people defied God and were confounded in their speech; at Pentecost, the people receive the Holy Spirit and acquire intelligibility.

There were **"visitors from Rome, both Jews and proselytes"** (Acts 2:10). At the time of Pentecost, the total population of the Roman Empire was about fifty million people, of whom as many as ten million were Jews or Judaizers, people who associated themselves with Judaism to some degree. Judaism was attractive to many people because of its pro-life values, good hygiene, and moral coherence. The Kosher laws made it difficult for non-Jews to convert into full membership, but many God-fearing people strove to fulfill the Ten Commandments, read the Septuagint Greek translation of the Bible, attended synagogue services and even made pilgrimage to Jerusalem, where they could gather in the Court of the Gentiles, the outer courtyard of the Temple. Christianity would offer to these God-Fearers the means to achieve full membership in the people of God, without having to adopt Mosaic law in its entirety.

11

"We hear them telling in our own tongues the mighty works of God" (Acts 2:11). Luke uses two words to describe the gift of language, received on Pentecost Sunday. In Acts 2:4 and 11, he uses the word *Glossa* (tongue), but in verse eight, Luke uses *Dialectos* (regional language). The gift has a purpose, which is communication. Whereas at the Tower of Babel, God confused human speech to thwart people's ability to conspire against the good, through the Pentecostal gift, God restores intelligibility, so that empowered by the Spirit, people would be able to work together for the good. The gift of languages exists to make possible the greater gift of the unity of the church. The people marveled on the first Pentecost because they could understand, not just because they were impressed at the apostles' linguistic abilities. The gift of understanding is greater than the gift of tongues, and God gives some people the ability to proclaim His Word precisely so that all may understand.

The church has continued to exercise the gift of tongues down through the centuries. The Roman church has continued to use Latin; the Russian church still uses Old Church Slavonic; the Greek church uses New Testament Greek and not modern Greek in their liturgy; churches in the Near East and India continue to use Aramaic, Jesus' language, in their liturgies. These ritual languages have not stood as an impediment to understanding, because of the gift of Pentecost. Saint Teresa of Avila, one of the best-read women of her day, did not fail to understand the things of God because the liturgy was celebrated in Latin, which she could not understand, rather than in her native tongue, Spanish. She is now recognized as a doctor of the church, because the Holy Spirit taught her the things of God.

Today the Church exercises the Pentecostal gift by approving the celebration of the liturgy in every language of the world. Even as Christians hear the Word of God and the preaching in their own languages, we still rely upon the Holy Spirit to teach us the meaning of the words. The Holy Spirit continues to instruct and inspire us when the Mass is in the vernacular or an ancient language.

"Day by day attending the temple together and breaking bread in their homes, they partook of food with glad and generous hearts" (Acts 2:46). With these words, Luke describes the liturgical life of the early church. They continued to worship in the temple, because God did not abandon the temple on Pentecost Sunday. The disciples themselves become temples of the Holy Spirit, but they continued to revere and present themselves before the sanctuary of God in Jerusalem. In this way, they demonstrated that there is no possible contradiction between the personal and the communal movements of grace.

While continuing to celebrate the temple rituals in public, the primitive Christians also celebrated their communal liturgies at home. For the first three centuries of the church's history, the home was the church. Only after Emperor Constantine made Christianity legal in the Roman Empire did the church, which is people, begin erecting large churches out of stone. Many wonderful churches would come into being, including the great Romanesque and Gothic cathedrals, some of the finest achievements in the history of architecture. When the people of God are in church, however, the people are the church, and the building is the halo around them.

Luke uses the term "breaking bread" to describe the primeval liturgy. During the Last Supper, Jesus had "broken bread" with His disciples and given them His Body and Blood (Luke 22:19). Later, on the road to Emmaus, the Risen Jesus had revealed Himself to the traveling disciples in the "breaking of the bread" (Luke 24:30). Clearly the earliest celebrations of the primitive church were Eucharistic. Jesus had told them to "do this in remembrance of me" (Luke 22:19), and there was no gap of forgetfulness between Jesus' command and the disciples' obedience. From the beginning, the disciples remembered, not year by year as in the old Passover, but "day by day." They had to remember the One to whom they would testify in Jerusalem, Samaria, and throughout the whole world.

1. How long did Jesus remain with His disciples after His Resurrection? Acts 1:1–3

* What did Jesus command the apostles to do? Acts 1:4–5

2. What do the apostles ask Jesus? Acts 1:6

3. According to Jesus, what is the purpose of the present time? Acts 1:7, CCC 672

4. What did Jesus promise and what did He commission? Acts 1:8

A New Pentecost

In February 1967, at Duquesne University in Pittsburgh, the only Spiritan University in the world, some college students on retreat renewed their Confirmation promises. They were overcome by the power of the Holy Spirit and began to pray in tongues, experiencing great joy. Similar experiences happened to others in different places, and soon the Catholic Charismatic Renewal was born.

Life in the Spirit Seminars led participants to renounce sin, accept the saving power of Jesus in their lives, and desire a greater outpouring of the Holy Spirit. Clergy and lay people would lay hands on others to pray for the "Baptism in the Holy Sprit" and healing. The spiritual gifts described in 1 Corinthians 12:1–11 flourished in people's lives. Some people found grace to turn away from serious sin patterns and return to the sacraments. Many found that Sacred Scripture came alive for them. Prayer meetings sprang up in church basements and school halls, in which joyful music, praying in tongues, and prophetic utterances were commonplace.

Inspired by Acts 2:44–45, many people empowered by the Holy Spirit sought to share their lives in a committed way. Covenant Communities sprang up around the world, in which people would live near others who were trying to live gospel values in a radical way, to pray, and support one another. Youthful zeal and enthusiasm resulted in trial and errors, and yet the experience of living in Christian community continues to be a profound blessing for many families and single adults.

Leon Joseph Suenens, Cardinal of Malines–Brussels, Belgium, visited some Charismatic Communities in the United States and recognized "Pentecostal grace at work." At his invitation, 10,000 Charismatic Catholics gathered at Saint Peter's Basilica in Rome in 1975 for an International Charismatic Conference. Pope Paul VI greeted the pilgrims saying, "The Church and the world need more than ever that the miracle of Pentecost should continue in history. How could this spiritual renewal not be good fortune for the Church and the world?" Later, in 1979, Pope John Paul II said "I am convinced that this movement is a sign of the Spirit's action …a very important component in the total renewal of the Church."

And in 1997, the United States bishops pronounced: "We, the United States Bishops Ad Hoc Committee on the Catholic Charismatic Renewal, want to affirm again all those Catholics involved in this movement of the Holy Spirit in our day. We, likewise, encourage them in their efforts to renew the life of the Church."

Following the "Baptism in the Holy Spirit," people were drawn to prayer and service. Soon many were volunteering to visit the sick, to serve the parish in music ministry, catechesis, youth ministry, marriage preparation, prison ministry, and other areas of need. Evangelism flourished as people eagerly shared what the Lord had done in their own lives. Dramatic stories of healings and deliverance from addictions and serious sin patterns touched the lives of the curious and the seekers. Stories paralleled those found in the Acts of the Apostles, as in a New Pentecost.

On June 3, 1998, Pope John Paul II addressed members of Charismatic Covenant Communities: "Certainly, your own charism leads you to direct your life toward a special 'intimacy' with the Holy Spirit. A survey of thirty years of the history of the Catholic Charismatic Renewal shows that you have helped many people to rediscover the presence and power of the Holy Spirit in their lives, and in the life of the Church—a rediscovery which in many of them has led to a faith in Christ filled with joy and enthusiasm, a great love of the Church and a generous dedication to her mission. ... I was deeply touched by the spirit of recollection and prayer, the atmosphere of joy and celebration in the Lord, which marked that event, a true gift of the Holy Spirit in the year dedicated to him. It was an intense moment of ecclesial communion and a demonstration of the unity of the many different charisms, which distinguish the ecclesial movements and new communities."

Eight years later to the day, Pope Benedict XVI said: "You belong to different peoples and cultures and represent here all the members of the Ecclesial Movements and New Communities, spiritually gathered round the Successor of Peter to proclaim the joy of believing in Jesus Christ and to renew the commitment to be faithful disciples in our time. ... Let us pray to God the Father, therefore, through Our Lord Jesus Christ, in the grace of the Holy Spirit, so that the celebration of Pentecost may be like an ardent flame and a blustering wind for Christian life and for the mission of the whole Church. I place the intentions of your Movements and Communities in the heart of the Most Blessed Virgin Mary, present in the Upper Room together with the Apostles; may she be the one who implores God to grant them. Upon all of you I invoke an outpouring of the gifts of the Spirit, so that in our time too, we may have the experience of a renewed Pentecost" (Pope Benedict XVI, June 3, 2006).

The last three popes have witnessed the fruit of the New Pentecost, evident in transformed lives dedicated to profound service in the Church and have provided encouragement and pastoral wisdom. Many books have been written about healings, miracles, and changed lives. Many more "glory stories" remain unwritten.

John Kazanjian, a Californian of Armenian descent, was taught to hate the Turks who were responsible for the slaughter of 1.5 million Armenians in 1915. After John experienced an outpouring of the Holy Spirit, he moved to Ann Arbor, where he met and married Michelle. Twenty-five years after experiencing this empowerment in the Holy Spirit, John, Michelle and their five daughters make frequent trips to Turkey to evangelize Turks and Muslims and to pray over Christians for the Baptism of the Holy Spirit. John's college-aged daughter Ani wants to study Arabic, so she can better evangelize people in the Middle East. Even though John is a businessman with many family responsibilities, he spends his own money and vacation time to travel back to the homeland of his parents to bring the Gospel message to others. The Holy Spirit has replaced hatred with Christian love. The Holy Spirit has given John and his family missionary zeal. John's and Michelle's and their children's love for Jesus and their hearts for evangelism demonstrate the fruit of the New Pentecost. God's Word is living and true. The miracle of Pentecost continues to enfold in this present age.

5. Where did Jesus of Nazareth go?

Acts 1:9	
CCC 659	
CCC 665	

6. Who was in the Upper Room and what were they doing? Acts 1:12–14

7. With whom does the Holy Spirit unite us and by what means? CCC 2673

* Explain Mary's *"Fiat."* CCC 2617

8. Who established criteria for replacing Judas? Explain the criteria. Acts 1:15–22

9. Describe the drama in Acts 2:1–13.

10. When did you receive the full outpouring of the Holy Spirit? CCC 1302

* What has the Holy Spirit done in your life? CCC 1303, 1308, 1309

11. According the Old Testament prophecies, what will the Holy Spirit do?

Joel 2:28a	
Joel 2:28b	
Acts 2:17–21	
CCC 715	

12. What does Saint Peter tell about Jesus? Acts 2:22–24, CCC 640

13. How was Jesus raised from the dead? Acts 2:24, CCC 648

14. Where is Hades and why did Jesus descend to the dead? Acts 2:27, CCC 633

15. Where did Jesus go after His Ascension? Acts 2:32–36, CCC 663

16. How did the listeners respond to Peter's words? Acts 2:36–37

17. What does Peter tell the people to do, and what does he promise? Acts 2:38

18. What does the Holy Spirit do?

John 14:26	
CCC 1287	
CCC 1433	

19. Why do we say the Church is apostolic?   CCC 857

20. How did the early Christians live? Acts 2:42–47

Acts 2:42–47	
CCC 2624	

* Have you ever had a personal experience of the power of the Holy Spirit in your life? If not, pray that the Holy Spirit would manifest Himself to you. You might also want to ask others to pray with you for more of the Holy Spirit in your life.

Chapter 2

Peter and John – AD 30
Acts 3–5

**But Peter said, "I have no silver and gold, but I give you what I have;
in the name of Jesus Christ of Nazareth, rise and walk."**
Acts 3:6

Peter, who already restored the Twelve (Acts 1:15), and is the spokesman for the Twelve (Acts 2:14), teams up with the apostle John in the succeeding chapters of Acts. Instead of surrounding himself with senior apostles, Peter takes as his collaborator the youngest. Though counterintuitive, such an association grows naturally out of the interactions already demonstrated among the Twelve.

Whenever Jesus appears in the gospels with four apostles, they are Peter, Andrew, James, and John. These four fellow fishers on the Sea of Galilee (Luke 5:10) received their call on the same day (Mark 1:19), and later jointly interrogated Jesus while contemplating the temple (Mark 13:3). These four stand together at the head of all the apostolic lists. The most common sequence pairs Simon with his brother Andrew and James with his brother John: "The names of the twelve apostles are these: first Simon, who is called Peter, and Andrew his brother; James the son of Zebedee, and John his brother" (Matthew 10:2). As characteristic of the Gospel of Matthew, this kind of listing is very Semitic, because the family relationship bestows the name and the identity upon these men. The older brother bears the father's name, and the younger brother is mentioned second. So we know that Peter is the older brother to Andrew, and James is the older brother to John.

Mark's gospel is under Roman influence and so deviates from the familial structure and relegates Andrew to fourth place. "Simon whom he surnamed Peter; James the son of Zebedee and John the brother of James, whom he surnamed Boanerges, that is, sons of thunder; Andrew and …" (Mark 3:16–18). This sequence reflects the fact that when Jesus appears with only three of the apostles, they are usually Peter, James, and John—at the inner chamber of the home of Jairus (Matthew 5:37), at the Transfiguration (Mark 9:2, Matthew 17:1, Luke 9:28), and at the garden of agony (Mark 14:33).

Luke, the careful researcher with a scientific mind, gives two different sequences. In Luke's gospel, he follows the usual order. "He called his disciples, and chose from them twelve, whom he named apostles: Simon, whom he named Peter, and Andrew his brother, and James and John" (Luke 6:13–14). But, at the beginning of Acts, he relegates Andrew to fourth position, and moves John up to second: "Peter and John and James and Andrew" (Acts 1:13).

Peter and John had reclined near Jesus at the Last Supper (John 13:23–24) and were the first two apostles to witness the empty tomb (John 20:2). Their common love for the Lord, both before and after His Resurrection, forms the basis of their working relationship, placing them together at the head of the apostolic hierarchy. Luke does not mention what the other apostles were doing at that time, but they were probably paired up as well for the office of witnessing. Jesus had sent out His twelve apostles two-by-two *(duo duo)* [Mark 6:7], and had likewise sent out His seventy-two disciples somewhat two-by-two *(ana duo duo)* [Luke 10:1]. This pattern reappears in the Acts of the Apostles, where the missionaries go out in pairs. Paul travels on his first mission journey with Barnabas (Acts 13:2) and on his second with Silas (Acts 15:40). Barnabas then teamed off with Mark (Acts 15:39).

The reason for all this double witnessing is quite simple. The Torah requires two or three witnesses in a capital case. "On the evidence of two witnesses or of three witnesses he that is to die shall be put to death; a person shall not be put to death on the evidence of one witness" (Deuteronomy 17:6). Later in the same book the same standard of proof is extended to all charges, even those not involving the death penalty. "A single witness shall not prevail against a man. … only on the evidence of two witnesses, or of three witnesses, shall a charge be sustained" (Deuteronomy 19:15). Paul quotes the last half of this verse in the context of his complaints against the Corinthians (2 Corinthians 13:1). Jesus also applied the standard of multiple witnesses for disputes within the church (Matthew 18:16).

Even Jesus did not give witness alone but had the corroborative testimony of His Father (John 8:17–18). Since the apostles are witnessing to the nations in a matter of life and death—the death and Resurrection of Jesus, and the life and death of every human being on the face of the earth—they do not expect anyone to give assent to their preaching without this double testimony. At first there are enough witnesses to the Risen Lord that they can go out in pairs. Later, one eyewitness seems to be teamed up with a non-eyewitness, as in the case with Paul (considered an eye-witness because of his vision) and his partners.

"Peter and John were going up to the temple at the hour of prayer, the ninth hour" (Acts 3:1). Jews throughout the world offered prayers three times a day towards Jerusalem (Daniel 6:10). The ninth hour was three o'clock in the afternoon, the third and last prayer time of the day, because for Jews sunset meant the end of one day and the beginning of the next. Jews in Jerusalem prayed toward the temple, and those in the temple prayed toward the sanctuary. At both the morning hour and the afternoon hour, the Levitical priests offered sacrifices—a lamb (Exodus 29:39) and an ephah of flour (Leviticus 6:20). The historian Josephus says that these sacrifices were so important that the priests continued to offer them even while the Romans were storming the temple (*Antiquities of the Jews,* xiv.4.3).

Peter and John enter the temple from the east, through the principal entry, which gave direct access from the Kidron Valley into the temple precinct. Herod called this the Susa Gate, because it pointed east toward Mesopotamia. Luke uses the more common designation, the Beautiful Gate, in Hebrew *sha'ar yafe,* in Greek *he horaia pylae* (Acts 3:2), in Arabic *al-bab al-jamil.* Crusaders called this the Golden Gate, *Porta Aurea,* because the rising sun causes the stones to shine. Sulayman the Magnificent rebuilt the walls of Jerusalem in the 16th century AD, and today the east entrance is a double gate, the left entry called The Gate of Salvation, *bab ar-ramah,* and the right The Gate of Expectation, *bab at-tobe.*

Luke seems to imply that the healing of the beggar lame from birth took place at the time of the Festival of Tabernacles. Even today, Orthodox Jews wait for the Messiah under the Golden Gate in the Kidron Valley during that feast at the end of the fall harvest. Peter's sermon alludes to that belief. "Repent, therefore, and turn again, that your sins may be blotted out, that times of refreshing may come from the presence of the Lord, and that he may send the Christ appointed for you, Jesus, whom heaven must receive until the time for establishing" (Acts 3:19–21).

"I have no silver and gold, but I give you what I have" (Acts 3:6). Jews considered the giving of alms an act of piety, as Jesus reconfirmed (Luke 11:41, 12:33). Jewish pilgrims entering the holy city would have seen the beggar, not as an inconvenience, but as an opportunity to fulfill a religious duty. Pilgrims were generous to beggars, and when Peter says, "I have no silver and gold," he does not mean to put the lame man off, but to offer a far greater gift, the healing of his body. This was a far superior act of piety, the making of another person whole. One of the signs for the Messianic age was the healing of the lame. Peter does not heal the beggar in his own name but "in the name of Jesus Christ of Nazareth," which in Peter's Aramaic was *Bishma' di Meshiha' Yeshua' di Nazaret.*

"Men of Israel, why do you wonder?" (Acts 3:12). Peter's first sermon took place on Pentecost Sunday outside the Upper Room on Mount Zion, near the Tomb of David. His second sermon takes place on the Feast of Booths on Mount Moriah, in the temple portico, called Solomon's Portico. These locations are of great Messianic importance, one associated with King David, founder of the Israelite royal house, and the other with Solomon, his son and builder of the first temple. Peter's first sermon had two parts, the first addressing "Men of Judea and all who dwell in Jerusalem" (Acts 2:14) and the second addressing "Men of Israel" (Acts 2:22). Peter expands his audience, first speaking to the smaller crowd of the Judeans, to whom he as a Galilean does not belong, and then the much larger crowd of all the Jews from everywhere on earth gathered in Jerusalem. The second sermon begins with the larger audience, to the "Men of Israel" (Acts 3:12).

"Moses said, 'The Lord your God will raise up for you a prophet'" (Acts 3:22). In the first sermon, Peter speaks of David not as a king, but as a prophet. "Brethren, I may say to you confidently of the patriarch David that he both died and was buried, and his tomb is with us to this day. Being therefore a prophet, and knowing that God had sworn with an oath to him that he would set one of his descendants upon his throne, he foresaw and spoke of the resurrection of the Christ, that he was not abandoned to Hades, nor did his flesh see corruption" (Acts 2:29–31). The passage even quotes two of the writings of David (Psalms 132:11 and 16:10). The second sermon stops just shy of calling Jesus Himself a prophet, a designation some had used during His lifetime (Matthew 16:14).

"**And they arrested them**" (Acts 4:3). At the end of Peter's second sermon, the authorities arrest Peter and John, the first of the apostles to endure imprisonment in the pages of Acts. The next day, the high priest convenes an inquiry, and Peter addresses those assembled with the words, "Rulers of the people and elders" (Acts 4:8). Peter's sermons just keep getting better, and this third sermon is a small jewel. At the core of the apostolic profession of faith is Peter's declaration made to Christ's own face —"You are the Christ" (Mark 8:29), —"The Christ of God" (Luke 9:20), —"You are the Christ, the Son of the living God" (Matthew 16:13). Eventually these early teachings and others will be codified in The Apostles' Creed, one of the simplest credal formulas of the early church.

The Apostles' Creed

I believe in God, the Father almighty, creator of heaven and earth.
I believe in Jesus Christ, his only Son, our Lord.
    He was conceived by the power of the Holy Spirit and born of the Virgin Mary.
    He suffered under Pontius Pilate, was crucified, died, and was buried.
    He descended to the dead. On the third day he rose again.
    He ascended into heaven, and is seated at the right hand of the Father.
    He will come again to judge the living and the dead.
I believe in the Holy Spirit, the holy catholic Church, the communion of saints,
    the forgiveness of sins, the resurrection of the body, and life everlasting. Amen.

Embedded in Peter's presentation is the verse, "This is the stone which was rejected by you builders, but which has become the head of the corner" (Psalm 118:22), which interestingly appears again in the First Letter of Peter (1 Peter 2:7). Of course, Jesus named Peter "rock" and now Peter calls Jesus "stone."

"**They arrested the apostles and put them in the common prison**" (Acts 5:18). Peter and John end up in prison a second time, and this time all the other apostles are with them. The Sanhedrin deliberate over their fate, and the apostles are exonerated and released through the intercession of the esteemed Rabbi Gamaliel, an important figure in the rise of rabbinic Judaism (Acts 5:34). Here the nascent Christian and Rabbinic movements support each other at a critical point in their early development. Gamaliel foreshadows the great Jewish and Christian leaders at the end of the Twentieth Century, who renounced the bad feeling that had accumulated for centuries and reached out a hand of friendship and to each other.

"**And every day in the temple and at home they did not cease teaching and preaching Jesus as the Christ**" (Acts 5:42). Just as Jesus had explained to the apostles "everything written about me in the law of Moses and the prophets and the psalms" (Luke 24:44), and "opened their minds to understand the scriptures" (Luke 24:45), so the apostles pass on to their followers the Christian interpretation of the Word of God. They held Bible study, and Peter would explain to them Psalm 118:22, in these words: "Come to him, to that living stone, rejected by men but in God's sight chosen and precious; and like living stones be yourselves built into a spiritual house, to be a holy priesthood, to offer spiritual sacrifices acceptable to God through Jesus Christ" (1 Peter 2:4–5).

John, after listening quietly to Peter for three chapters, finally opens his mouth and gives joint testimony with Peter (Acts 4:19). John is thus the second of the apostles to give testimony, but only in union with the teaching of Peter. Luke expresses high esteem in which he holds the apostle John by giving him such prominent mention at the beginning of Acts. Of the three synoptic evangelists (Matthew, Mark, and Luke), Luke is the one whose texts possess the most in common with the Gospel of John. These two factors seem to suggest that John, the youngest of the apostles, and Luke, a second-generation Christian, were well acquainted with one another.

After the death of his brother James (Acts 12:2), John never appears again in Acts. Tradition relates that he took the Blessed Mother to Ephesus and lived a long life there as the only apostle not to shed his blood for his testimony to the Lord. The authorities tried to kill him, but he survived and was exiled to the Island of Patmos. In his Gospel and three surviving letters, he never mentions his own name, because he wants to give Christ the glory. He calls himself only "the disciple whom the Lord loved" in his Gospel. When John died, his body was laid to rest in Ephesus, at the site of the Church of Saint John.

1. Explain the drama in Acts 3:1–10.

2. How was the lame beggar healed? Acts 3:11–16

3. What can you learn from these passages?

Mark 1:15	
Acts 3:19–21	
CCC 1427	

4. How can you find times of refreshment that come from the Lord?

Acts 3:19	
CCC 1425	
CCC 1426	

* When can you next plan to celebrate the Sacrament of Reconciliation?

5. Find a fulfillment of prophecy from these passages.

Deuteronomy 18:18–19	
Acts 3:22–26	

6. How did people respond to Peter's preaching? Acts 4:1–4

Acts 4:1–3	*Leaders*	
Acts 4:4	*People*	

7. What can you learn from the following passages?

Psalm 118:22	
Isaiah 28:16	
Acts 4:8–12	
1 Peter 2:6–8	

8. What did the leaders observe about Peter and John? Acts 4:13–16

9. How did Peter and John respond to the order to stop preaching? Acts 4:17–20

* Have you ever felt called to obey God, contrary to civil authorities?

10. After release from prison, for what did the apostles pray? Acts 4:23–30

11. How did God answer the apostles' prayer? Acts 4:31

12. Describe how the early Christians lived. Acts 4:32–37

13. How should Christians apply this passage to their lives today? CCC 952

* What possession of yours would be most difficult for you to share or give up?

14. Explain the drama in Acts 5:1–10.

15. What emotion followed the deaths of Ananias and Sapphira? Acts 5:11

16. How did the people respond to the apostles? Acts 5:12–16

17. Describe the situation in Acts 5:17–26.

18. What response did Peter give to the high priest? Acts 5:27–32

19. Who came to defend the apostles? What logic did he offer? Acts 5:33–39

20. What happened to the apostles and how did they respond? Acts 5:40–42

* How do you feel about witnessing to Christ and suffering for Him?

Chapter 3

The Diaconal Order — AD 31
Acts 6–7

**And as they were stoning Stephen, he prayed,
"Lord Jesus, receive my spirit."**
Acts 7:59

On October 18, 31 AD, intelligence reached the Emperor Tiberius on the Isle of Capri that the powerful tribune L. Aelius Sejanus, de facto ruler of the Empire for a number of years, was planning a coup d'etat. The Emperor sent out orders for Sejanus, his family and his followers to be slaughtered, and the pogrom took place. The future emperor Claudius then divorced his wife, Aelia, the sister of Sejanus.

Sejanus was anti-Semitic, and his fall made life easier for Jews throughout the Empire, and for Christians fresh opportunities arose for growth. Specifically, more Jews throughout the Roman Empire planned to make pilgrimage to Jerusalem on the high holydays. Many had been hesitant for a decade or longer to venture forth in hostile circumstances, and now many Jews plan to visit Jerusalem on Passover, Pentecost, and Booths in the following year. The result is a surge of pilgrims worshipping at the temple. Perhaps twice as many pilgrims are in Jerusalem this year than were there on Pentecost Sunday in the Year 29. The apostles continue preaching to the holyday throngs year-by-year, reaching new people, and the numbers exposed to their kerygma rise to new heights in Years 32, 33, and 34.

Thus the Fall of Sejanus is one of a number of circumstances favoring the early spread of this new movement, "The Way." More Jews than ever from the diaspora (Greek speaking world) find favorable conditions to go to Jerusalem on pilgrimage, and while there, many receive the gift of the Holy Spirit through the preaching of the Apostles. From the very first years, the Christian message reaches the Jews from around the world, and not just to the Jews dwelling in the Holy Land itself.

"The Hellenists murmured against the Hebrews" (Acts 6:1). By the sixth chapter of Acts, two parallel Christian communities seem to be taking shape, one Hebrew and the other Greek. The Hebrew community consists of Aramaic-speaking Jews native to the land both Judeans and Galileans, who did have slightly different dialects of Aramaic, but could understand each other satisfactorily, and hence could form a single community. The Greek community comprised diaspora Jews who had returned to the Holy Land. Jews throughout the Roman Empire spoke Greek, even those residing in the city of Rome itself. Hence the term "Greeks" here means not people of Hellenic race, but people of Hellenized speech.

The differences between the two groups were more than a matter of mere speech. Languages encapsulate culture. The Hebrew community was more provincial, centered on the Holy Land proper. The Greek community was more cosmopolitan, aware of trends in the larger world and sensitive to those issues. Their table talk differed both in language and in subject. The two communities shared one Lord, one faith, and one baptism, but they inhabited different cultural universes.

Modern theologians call this phenomenon *inculturation*—translating the Gospel into the milieu of a given society, enabling the values of Christianity to interact with the context in which people find themselves. From the earliest years, people from different cultures came to Jerusalem and discovered Jesus, but they did not cease to be "Parthians, Medes, Elamites," and so forth. They were not really foreigners, because as Jews they had the right to consider this their own land, but culturally they belonged to different worlds. The longer they stayed in Jerusalem, the more they adapted to the locality, but every year new immigrants were arriving and keeping the Greek synagogues Greek and the Roman synagogues Roman.

The apostles display true pastoral care in not relegating the Greek-speaking widows to second-class status behind the Hebrew-speaking widows. At stake here was not just the value of inclusiveness but the very catholicity of the church itself. If, at the very beginning, a two-tier Christianity had emerged, then the whole future history of the religion would have been doomed to a widening gap between the ins and the outs, the haves and the have-nots. Society always seems to separate itself out in this way, but the driving pastoral plan of the apostolic church tries to bridge those gaps, to create from many peoples one voice to proclaim one faith.

"It is not right that we should give up preaching the word of God in order to serve tables" (Acts 6:2). Banqueting provided the most important social setting for Greek and Roman society. The philosopher Plato entitled one of his dialogues "The Symposium," which in modern English means a round-table discussion but in the original Greek means a banquet including both food and the table talk. Plato and his friends reclined at table together and, during the course of the meal, discussed the major topics of the day, including the issues of philosophy.

While wealthy Greeks of both genders dined, their male slaves called "deacons" waited on them at table, delivering each course and taking away the used tableware. The deaconate in the church derives from this practice. The apostles determined that it was not right for them to wait on tables, at the expense of preaching the Gospel. So, they instituted a special order to serve people's practical needs.

"Diaconate" already existed as an implied aspect of apostleship. Jesus taught His disciples that just as He had come to serve and not to be served, so authority in the church should involve service. Jesus named all twelve of His apostles to service, and they later bequeath several aspects of that service to the diaconal order. Therefore, one might say that all apostles are deacons, but not all deacons are apostles.

The Church recognizes three major orders within the Sacrament of Holy Orders—deacon, priest, and bishop. The Church has always required priests to be ordained deacon first, and bishops to be ordained priest first. This invariable sacramental sequence demonstrates that all priests are deacons, and all bishops are priests. The bishop possesses the fullness of the priesthood of Jesus Christ, and the diaconate and priesthood are kinds of participation in that one priesthood.

Harmony between the orders is essential to the unity of the Church. Within any parish the deacons must collaborate with their pastor. Within a diocese, the priests must work with their ordinary bishop. Within the universal Church, the bishops must function in unity with the holder of the petrine office, the Pope. The one priesthood of Jesus Christ deserves no less than this.

"Pick out from among you seven men" (Acts 6:3). The apostles ask the congregation to nominate the seven deacons, who are then formally presented. The apostles lay hands on them and pray over them. These formal stages continue as Church practice today, in the process of candidacy leading up to the rite of ordination. The rector of the seminary presents the candidate to the bishop, who then asks the congregation whether they approve of the ordination. Then the bishop prays the consecratory prayer and imposes his hands on the candidate, thus conferring the sacred order.

Some of the apostles had Greek names in addition to Hebrew ones, but the first deacons in Acts 6:5–6 all have strictly Greek names:
- — Stephen means "crown".
- — Philip means "horse lover".
- — Prochorus means "dance master".
- — Nicanor means "conqueror".
- — Timon means "honorable".
- — Parmenas means "steadfast".
- — Nicolaus means "conqueror of peoples".

The laying on of hands appears often in the New Testament, sometimes in connection with healing and sometimes with appointment to an office. The rabbis of that time imposed hands on their students as a kind of graduation ceremony, empowering the student to go out and become a master. Jesus laid hands on His disciples, who went out and laid hands on their disciples, and so on, down to the present day. The Church sees the continuity of orders in the Church as going back to Jesus Himself. Every priest or deacon knows which bishop ordained him, and the bishops of today are literally successors of the apostles, in an unbroken episcopal line. When the bishop teaches, rules, and sanctifies, he does so by virtue of his apostolic function, and each priest or deacon teaches, administers and sanctifies by virtue of the faculties given him by the bishop.

"And Stephen said: Brethren and fathers, hear me" (Acts 7:2). Although deacons came into being seemingly for the sake of waiting on tables, they soon begin to serve in other ministerial capacities with signal distinction. Stephen proffers a lengthy speech displaying a dazzling command of biblical history and then becomes the first person to give his life for his belief in Christ Crucified. Through Stephen, the new order of deacon distinguishes itself for all time, for a deacon becomes a first martyr.

In the year AD 258, Pope Sixtus II was martyred along with the seven deacons who assisted him in the administration of the Church of Rome. Five of the martyred deacons have Latin names:
— Januarius means "door keeper".
— Magnus means "great".
— Vincent means "conquering".
— Stephen means "crowned" in Greek.
— Agapitus means "beloved" in Greek.
— Felicissimus means "most happy".
— Lawrence means "honored".

"Lord, do not hold this sin against them" (Acts 7:9). Stephen demonstrates true forgiveness, conforming the Christian martyr with Jesus, who said from the cross, "Father, forgive them, for they know not what they do" (Luke 23:34). Just as in the case of Judaism, Christian remembrance is more than a mere mental process but rather a whole way of life. When the Christian martyrs give their lives for Christ, they show that they remember Him and they show it with their blood. The Maccabees, Hebrew martyrs, pioneered this path. The Maccabees shed blood for their faith in a future resurrection; the Christian martyrs shed their blood for their faith in a resurrection already begun in the Person of Jesus.

Martyr in Greek means "witness." The Christian martyr gives witness to Christ through the giving of his or her life, and every Christian is called to give witness and to conform his life to Christ. Since Christ gave His life for everyone else, the martyr unto death has been in a sense most perfectly conformed to the pattern of Christ's death and rising. For this reason, many of the martyrs prayed for the gift of being able to give their lives for Christ. Saint Jean de Brebeuf, a French Jesuit who became one of the protomartyrs of North America, said a special prayer every day for the last years of his life, begging God to grant him the grace of martyrdom. God granted him the gift of martyrdom alongside his confrere Gabriel Lalemant on March 15, 1649 in what is now New York State.

"What shall I offer back to you, O my Lord Jesus, for all that you have given me? I shall take up the cup and invoke your name. Therefore, I vow in the sight of your eternal Father and of the Holy Spirit, in the sight of your most holy Mother and of her most chaste spouse Joseph, before the Angels, Apostles and Martyrs, and of my spiritual father Ignatius and of Francis Xavier. I vow, I say, to you, O my Lord Jesus, that if ever to me your unworthy servant the grace of martyrdom should be mercifully offered by you, I shall not defer that grace; so that in future I should never allow myself the wish either to decline occasions which offer themselves of dying for you (unless I judge that it would be for your greater glory) or not to accept joyfully the blow of death already inflicted. To you, therefore, O my Lord Jesus, I gladly offer my blood and body and spirit already from this day, so that I may die, if you so grant, for you who deigned to die for me. Grant that I may live in such a manner that I may die just as you wish me to. So, Lord, may I take this cup, and invoke your name: Jesus, Jesus, Jesus."

1. Describe the problem that arose in the early church. Acts 6:1–2

2. What solution was found, and by whom? Acts 6:3–4

3. List the first seven deacons of the church. Acts 6:4–5

4. What happens in the following passages?

Acts 6:6–7	
1 Timothy 4:14	

5. Explain the three degrees of the Sacrament of Holy Orders.

Bishop	CCC 1555 1556 1557 1558
Priest	CCC 1563 1564 1565 1566
Deacon	CCC 1569 1570 1571

* Recall a bishop, priest, and deacon who ministered to you in a special way. Pray for each of them and write a note thanking one of them.

6. Describe the deacon Stephen. Acts 6:8–10, 15

7. What was plotted against Stephen? Acts 6:11–14

8. Stephen begins his discourse with what story? Acts 7:2–8

9. Compare two other reports of this story.

Genesis 12–17	
Hebrews 11:8–19	

10. How does Stephen continue his discourse? Acts 7:9–16

11. What can you learn from the following passages?

Exodus 2:1–10	
Acts 7:17–22	
Hebrews 11:23–26	

12. What happened when Moses was 40 years old? Acts 7:23–29

13. What happened when Moses was 80 years old? Acts 7:30–36

14. How did the people of Israel relate to Moses? Acts 7:35–41

15. How did God respond? Amos 5:25–27, Acts 7:42–43

16. How was God present among the people?

Acts 7:44–46	
Acts 7:47	
Isaiah 66:1–2	

17. What criticism is made in these verses and by whom?

Matthew 23:31–34	
Acts 7:51–53	

18. What and Whom did Stephen see?

Matthew 26:64	
Acts 7:55–56	
Revelation 1:13–16	

19. How was Stephen martyred and who was there? Acts 7:57–58, 8:1

20. What was Stephen's final act in life? Acts 7:59–60

* Is there someone you need to forgive? Pray for the grace of forgiveness.

Chapter 4

Philip the Deacon — AD 33
Acts 8

**Then Philip opened his mouth, and beginning with this scripture
he told him the good news of Jesus.**
Acts 8:35

The name Philip became quite common in the Mediterranean world after the reign of Philip I of Macedonia, father of Alexander the Great. Philip means a "lover of horses" (phil-hippos), and indeed the Greeks were noted for fine cavalry. A great bas-relief from the Pantheon in Athens, now in the British Museum, shows two teenagers astride spirited ponies on the fringes of the panathenaic procession.

Near the Macedonian city of Philippi, a very important battle took place on the 23rd of October in 42 BC, when Marc Antony and Octavian Caesar defeated Brutus and Cassius, the assassins of Julius Caesar. The victors appointed Herod the Great ruler of the Holy Land, and in gratitude Herod named two of his sons Philip (Luke 3:1; 3:19). For the next hundred years the Julian and Herodian families ruled together, the Julians over the empire and the Herodians over the Holy Land. Both dynasties fancied themselves Hellenistic monarchs, and so Herod, though not Greek himself, gave his children Greek names.

Two followers of Jesus bear the Greek appellation Philip. One of the original twelve apostles (Acts 1:13) is named Philip, and a member of the first seven deacons (Acts 6:5) also bears the name Philip.

Philip the Apostle

All lists of the twelve apostles given in the Bible place Philip in the important fifth position, right after the two pairs of brothers, Peter and Andrew, and James and John. The evangelist John shows a special interest in this apostle, and reveals every detail otherwise known about him:

— Philip the Apostle came from the town of Bethsaida
  (John 1:44; 12:21).
— Right after answering the call of Jesus, he went to find his friend
  Nathaniel and told him to "Come and see" (John 1:46).
— Before feeding the five thousand, Jesus interrogated Philip about how
  they could buy bread to feed all the people (John 6:5).
— Some Greeks asked Philip for an introduction to Jesus (John 12:21).
— At the Last Supper, Philip asked Jesus to show them the Father
  (John 14:8–9).

Philip the Deacon

In his list of the seven deacons, Luke puts Philip in second place right after Stephen (Acts 6:5) and then provides all the information known about him:

— Philip led the mission to Samaria and worked miracles there Acts 8:5–7).
— He baptized many, letting the Apostles confirm them in the Spirit (Acts 8:16).
— An angel appeared to Philip in a dream, directing him to go down to the desert road near Gaza (Acts 8:26).
— Philip evangelized and baptized the Ethiopian eunuch (Acts 8:38).
— The Spirit whisked Philip away to Azotus (Acts 8:39–40).
— Twenty-five years later, Philip offered hospitality to Paul in Caesarea, by which time he had four unmarried prophetic daughters (Acts 21:8).

Already during Jesus' lifetime, Philip the Apostle showed himself to be a bridge to the larger Greek world. Later, Philip the Deacon evangelizes both to the north and south. What these two Philips have in common, in addition to their shared Greek name, is a solicitude to the external relationship of Christianity to the outer world.

Chapter 8 of Acts does not state clearly which Philip went to Samaria and Gaza, the apostle or the deacon. Both Philips were mentioned earlier in the book, the deacon two chapters before and the apostle five chapters before that. Following the grammatical and interpretive rule called *parataxis*, one should refer to the nearer antecedent, in this case the deacon. Like Stephen before him, Philip assumes new ministerial roles that were not clear at the time the deacons were appointed. For three chapters in a row, the book called "The Acts of the Apostles" has taken a little turn and become the "Acts of the Deacons."

The Outreach to Samaria — Before ascending into heaven, Jesus commissioned the apostles to witness to Him in Samaria (Acts 1:8). This presented a grave challenge, "for Jews have no dealings with Samaritans" (John 4:9). The first seemingly impossible mission faced by the early church was building a bridge to Samaria. Interestingly, a member of the new diaconal order spearheads this operation. Earlier, in the public ministry of Jesus Himself, the foundation had been laid for this work. Several times Jesus spoke approvingly of Samaritans, telling the parable of the "Good Samaritan," conversing with them in public, and healing their sick. Jesus praised the cured Samaritan leper who returned to give Him thanks. Jesus wanted this thrust of His ministry to continue in the work of the apostolic church, and He promised that the "fields are already white for harvest" (John 4:35).

Who were the Samaritans? In 722 BC, the Assyrian ruler Shalmaneser captured the city of Samaria, capital of the Northern Kingdom of Israel, and carried away 27,290 citizens. The Assyrians practiced a form of cultural genocide by moving populations around and mixing them with each other, so that, removed from their own lands and interspersed with foreigners, they would intermarry and lose their own unique religious and cultural customs. To replace the Israelite exiles, Shalmaneser settled non-Hebrew peoples from elsewhere in his empire. These Gentiles made this territory their own and intermarried with the remaining Israelite population, producing the mixed race later called Samaritan.

After the Judeans began returning from exile in 539 BC, their Samaritan cousins welcomed them eagerly and offered to help rebuild Jerusalem and the temple. They were rejected because of their racial impurity. An excommunicated Jewish priest fled to Samaria and established the Levitical priesthood among them, bringing them a copy of the Torah, which they accepted. They built their own temple in the city of Samaria, which the Jews destroyed, and so they build another temple on Mount Gerizim, which the Jewish high priest John Hyrcanus destroyed. By Jesus' time, they had a simple altar erected on the mountain, and conducted their services out-of-doors, including the high holydays of Passover, Pentecost, and Booths.

Samaritans, like Jews, were called spiritually to their cultic center in the Holy Land by the same Mosaic law of pilgrimage (Deuteronomy 16:16–17). Only the place of pilgrimage differed between the two peoples—the nature and times of pilgrimage remained the same. While the population of Jerusalem swelled to three or four times normal three times a year on the high holydays, on those same days a similar, though smaller, phenomenon occurred in Samaria around Mount Gerizim. Two pilgrimage centers, not very far apart, filled with pilgrims on festivals. The potential for conflict between Jews and Samaritans was greater around pilgrimage time because of the extensive movement of people and the presence of religious fanatics among the pilgrims. The Roman Prefect spent the holydays at the Antonia Fortress in Jerusalem, by far the larger pilgrimage site. Nonetheless, he had to also keep watch on what was happening at Mount Gerizim at the same time. Josephus describes what difficulty Pilate had maintaining control over both pilgrimage centers, which led to his withdrawal from Palestine (*Antiquities of the Jews*, 18:4).

The Samaritan Diaspora — Evidence demonstrates that Samaritans, like Jews, were scattered throughout the Mediterranean world. Josephus noted the presence of a Samaritan community in Egypt (Antiquities 11.345, 12.7, 13.74), and the Jewish pilgrim Obadia of Bertinor found fifty households of Samaritans at Cairo, compared with 650 Jewish ones, in the year 1487. In 1968 excavations at Salonika yielded the only verifiable Samaritan diaspora synagogue, with inscriptions from the Fourth Century AD. Also, in 1970 Philippe Bruneau published two inscriptions from the Second Century BC left on the Island of Delos by "the Israelites who make offerings to hallowed Mount Gerizim."

Although Luke narrates the mission to Samaria immediately after the martyrdom of Stephen, contacts with Samaria may have begun already. The speech of Stephen before the Sanhedrin (Acts 7:2–50) reflects Samaritan hermeneutics, in that he quotes favorite Samaritan texts and excludes any reference to the Davidic Messiah or Solomonic Temple. The native tradition of Abul-Fath claims that Stephen himself was a Samaritan. His Greek name and appearance among the deacons in Jerusalem identify him rather with Diaspora Jews who have returned to Palestine. But the Samaritan tone of Stephen's speech indicates that the Hellenists have already forged links to Samaria.

Samaritans were not welcome in Jerusalem nor were Jews welcome in Gerizim, but God-fearing pagans could visit both. "The Court of the Gentiles" formed the gigantic antechamber to the Jerusalem temple, and any sincere person could enter to worship and listen to the teachings. Huge numbers of Gentiles admired Judaism and some went on devotional pilgrimage to Jerusalem. Other, smaller numbers of Gentiles admired Samaritanism and were drawn to Gerizim. Religious syncretism flourished in the Roman world, and the pagan mind found no contradiction in visiting various shrines. Nothing prevented the curious and open-minded Gentile visitors from visiting both shrines. In fact, after months of dangerous travel to reach the Holy Land, the efficient pilgrim would see as much as he could.

The Hellenist deacons were primarily responsible for the opening to Samaria, because they knew people there. Some people from Alexandria had settled in Jerusalem, and some had settled in Samaria. Not bound by the centuries-old antagonisms of the local people, they formed a social bridge where none other existed, and Christianity marched over that bridge in answer to the missionary imperative of Jesus. The Greeks made it possible for Jews and Samaritans to meet together in Christianity, after six centuries of conflict.

Jesus foresaw and prophesied this. With Mount Gerizim looming overhead and the plain below filled with the encampments of pilgrims to the festival from around the world, one recalls the words of Jesus, "One sows and another reaps" (John 4:37). Samaritanism itself, the Gerizim cult, has sown, just as Judaism has, what Christianity will reap. The "worship in spirit and truth" will harvest what both Gerizim and Jerusalem have planted.

"They sent to them Peter and John" (Acts 8:14). First Stephen laid the groundwork, then Philip spearheaded, and finally Peter and John confirm the mission to Samaria. Peter and John appear together this one last time in the text of Acts, in the context of the mission to Samaria. Until that point, their ministry was limited to Jerusalem (the first part of Jesus' commission on Ascension Thursday). The apostles, sensing the importance of the Samaritan mission, send the senior and beloved apostles as a team in an official pastoral visit. Just as Pope Paul VI visited Africa to confirm the church there, and Pope John Paul II visited his native Poland while still under communist occupation, and Pope Benedict XVI revisited his native Germany, Peter chooses Samaria for the first papal visit of all time. Before Paul even became a Christian, Peter had already visited Samaria.

Acts gives the picture that the Christian movement remained safely within the parameters of Judaism so long as its proselytizing took place within the context of the Jews and Godfearers who attended the Temple on pilgrimage for the high holydays. There is no apparent reaction against the apostles for baptizing three thousand of them on the first Pentecost (Acts 2:41), and the apostles are able to continue teaching in the temple daily

(Acts 2:46). As long as Christianity was subservient to the Temple cult, she was even closer to Jewish orthopraxy than the Essene monks were, and she was able to proselytize within the highly diverse Judaism of the First Century.

Judaism was a big enough religion to embrace Christianity as long as it was tied to pilgrimage to Jerusalem. But Christianity was not small enough to limit its proselytizing only to those who made the Temple their spiritual home. The cutting edge of this clash of expectations comes with the mission to the Samaritans. Contained within this conflict, in the issues that led to the martyrdom of Stephen, are to be found in germ the whole program of Christian mission in the Book of Acts and until the end of time. In the mission to the Samaritans the church demonstrated that she was not inviting them to convert to Judaism but to join in a new worship in spirit and in truth.

The Apostolic Church of Ethiopia — The deacon Philip, who spearheaded the mission to the north, also makes an outreach southward. Once again, a Hellenist leads the way. Luke narrates the story in miraculous terms. Philip receives direction from an angel, takes a station on the desert road to Gaza, evangelizes and baptizes the Ethiopian eunuch, and then disappears from sight. This Ethiopian appears to be the first Gentile to become Christian without having first converted to Judaism. This certainly derives from the fact that Jewish tradition denied circumcision to people who were eunuchs. Unable to enter the People of God of the old dispensation, this man finds a place in the People of God of the new dispensation.

Ethiopia is the oldest Christian nation in Africa, with roots going back to apostolic times. The Ethiopian Coptic church has historic links with the Egyptian Coptic church, the eight million members of which form the largest Christian community in the Near East. Since the end of the colonial period, Christian conversion has increased dramatically throughout central and southern Africa. The continent now boasts many millions of Christians, and the forefather of them all appears right in the pages of the Acts of the Apostles.

> Our whole life must aspire to encounter Jesus as Philip encountered him, seeking to perceive in him God himself, the heavenly Father. If this commitment were lacking, we would be reflected back to ourselves as in a mirror and become more and more lonely! Philip teaches us instead to let ourselves be won over by Jesus, to be with him and also to invite others to share in this indispensable company; and in seeing, finding God, to find true life.
>
> Pope Benedict XVI, *General Audience*, September 6, 2006.

1. Describe the condition of the early church in Acts 8:1–3.

2. What can you learn about Saul from Acts 8:1, 3?

3. Where did Philip go, and what did he do? Acts 8:5

4. What resulted from Philip's efforts? Acts 8:6–8, 12

5. Who can receive Baptism? CCC 1226

6. How does the Church see Simon's occupation?

Acts 8:9–13	
CCC 2116	
CCC 2117	

* Identify some contemporary forms of magic that must be avoided.

7. Who do the apostles send to Samaria and for what purpose? Acts 8:14–17

8. What is the origin of the Sacrament of Confirmation? CCC 1288

9. Explain the significance of the "laying on of the hands."

Acts 8:17	
CCC 699	

10. What did Simon do? Acts 8:18–19

11. Explain the sin in Acts 8:18. CCC 2121

* Describe a contemporary example of the sin of simony.

12. How does Peter react to Simon's request? Acts 8:20–23

* Have you ever confronted anyone the way Peter did or been confronted?

13. How did Simon respond to Peter's words? Acts 8:24

14. Describe the messenger and message given to Philip. Acts 8:26

15. What was Philip's response? Acts 8:27

16. Describe the actor and activity in Acts 8:27–28.

17. What question does Philip pose to the Ethiopian? Acts 8:30

18. What can you learn from these passages? Who do they describe?

Isaiah 56:3–5	
Isaiah 53:7–8, 10–12	
1 Peter 1:10–12	

19. What did Philip do for the Ethiopian eunuch? Acts 8:35, 38

20. Describe Philip's departure. Acts 8:39–40

* Philip shared his faith. When have you shared your faith with someone?

Monthly Social Activity

This month, your small group will meet for coffee, tea, or a simple breakfast, lunch, or dessert in someone's home. Pray for this social event and for the host or hostess. Try, if at all possible, to attend.

After a short prayer and some time for small talk, write a few sentences about a "faith sharing experience" you had. Then write another sentence about how God brought it about. Try to share about this experience in a five-minute time frame.

Examples:

◆ *My friend Cynthia seemed suddenly more peaceful, more joyful, and less nervous. When I asked her what happened in her life, she shared with me her experience of coming to know God's love in a personal way. She then invited me to a Life in the Spirit Seminar.*

◆ *My brother-in-law had been a heavy drinker for years. Through AA, he was able to acknowledge his powerlessness over alcohol and put his trust in God. He shared with the family how good God has been in delivering him from his addiction to alcohol.*

◆ *My niece, Emma, wrote me a letter from college, asking me how I could remain so peaceful and confident. I wrote back explaining to her the changes that the Holy Spirit has made in my life, and encouraging her to seek out God's perfect will for her life.*

Chapter 5

The Conversion of Saul — AD 35
Acts 9; 22:4–16; 26:9–20; Galatians 1:13–24

And he (Saul) said, "Who are you Lord?"
And he said, "I am Jesus, whom you are persecuting."
Acts 9:5

The young man named Saul may have pushed northwards to Damascus, filled with zeal for the tradition of his ancestors, like many young people possessing not a single doubt about the strength of his cause. Before he reached his destination, however, God reduced him to a state of complete weakness and out of that humbling rose a new man, devoted to the very cause he had been persecuting. One way or the other, this young man was going to help launch a religion—if not rabbinic Judaism then mainline Christianity. The written records in Sacred Scripture reveal three clear facts about Saul's origin:

1) Saul was born in Tarsus, in the Roman province of Cilicia (Acts 9:11; 9:30; 11:25; 21:39, and 22:3). All the inhabitants of this city received the gift of Roman citizenship in the year 30 B.C. from the Emperor Augustus, whose childhood tutor Athenodoros was a native of Tarsus. As a result of his birth in Tarsus, Saul had all the rights of Roman citizenship, including the right to trial in the imperial courts (Acts 25:10–11).

2) Saul belonged to the tribe of Benjamin (Romans 11:1; Philippians 3:5), the smallest of the twelve tribes of Israel. The first king of Israel had been a Benjaminite by the name of Saul son of Kish, after whom Saul of Tarsus was named. Unfortunately, the word "saulos" means "limping" or "disabled" in the Greek. Perhaps the young man took on the name of Paul to avoid unwelcome puns on his Hebrew name.

3) Young Saul came to Jerusalem and studied in one of the best pharisaic schools, that of Rabbi Gamaliel (Acts 22:3), well known as one of founders of Rabbinic Judaism. Many Gamaliel sayings survive in rabbinic literature. Gamaliel appears in Acts as the voice of tolerance toward the early Christians, advising the men of Israel to leave them alone; for if their plan is of men, it will fail, but if of God, they will not be able to overthrow it (Acts 5:34). Saul did not emulate that moderate spirit, and became one of the staunch persecutors of Christians. He first appears holding the coats of those stoning to death the deacon Stephen, "And Saul was consenting to his death" (Acts 8:1). Saul accuses himself of arresting both men and women, and of voting in favor of the death penalty for them (Acts 26:10).

How did this man with such a background turn into the great missionary apostle of Christianity? The transformation was the work of God's grace and mercy. The New Testament recounts the story of Saul's conversion four times, once in the narrative of Luke (Acts 9:1–19), and three times in the words of Saul himself (Acts 22:4–16; Acts 26:9–20; and Galatians 1:13–24). A testimony repeated four times in Sacred Scripture is worthy of being carefully studied and compared, side-by-side.

THE BIBLICAL ACCOUNTS OF
THE CONVERSION OF SAUL

Acts 9:1–19	Acts 22:3–16
1 But Saul, still breathing threats and murder against the disciples of the Lord, went to the high priest 2 and asked him for letters to the synagogues at Damascus, so that if he found any belonging to the Way, men or women, he might bring them bound to Jerusalem.	3 "I am a Jew, born in Tarsus in Cilicia, but brought up in this city at the feet of Gamaliel, educated according to the strict … law of our fathers, being zealous for God as you all are this day. 4 I persecuted this Way to the death, binding and delivering to prison both men and women, 5 as the high priest and the council of elders bear me witness. From them I received letters to the brethren, and I journeyed to Damascus to take those who were there and bring them … to Jerusalem to be punished.
3 Now as he journeyed he approached Damascus, and suddenly a light from heaven flashed about him. 4 And he fell to the ground and heard a voice saying to him, "Saul, Saul, why do you persecute me?" 5 And he said, "Who are you, Lord?" And he said, "I am Jesus, whom you are persecuting; 6 but rise and enter the city, and you will be told what you are to do." 7 The men who were traveling with him stood speechless, hearing the voice but seeing no one. 8 Saul arose from the ground; and when his eyes were opened, he could see nothing: so they led him by the hand and brought him into Damascus. 9 And for three days he was without sight, and neither ate nor drank.	6 "As I made my journey and drew near to Damascus, about noon a great light from heaven suddenly shone about me. 7 And I fell to the ground and heard a voice saying to me, 'Saul, Saul, why do you persecute me?' 8 And I answered, 'Who are you, Lord?' And he said to me, 'I am Jesus of Nazareth whom you are persecuting.' 9 Now those who were with me saw the light but did not hear the voice of the one who was speaking to me. 10 And I said, 'What shall I do, Lord?' And the Lord said to me, 'Rise, and go into Damascus, and there you will be told all that is appointed for you to do.' 11 And when I could not see because of the brightness of that light, I was led by the hand by those who were with me, and came into Damascus …
17 So Ananias departed and entered the house. And laying his hands on him he said, "Brother Saul, the Lord Jesus who appeared to you on the road by which you came, has sent me that you may regain your sight and be filled with the Holy Spirit." 18 And immediately something like scales fell from his eyes and he regained his sight. Then he rose and was baptized, 19 and took food and was strengthened.	12 … Ananias, a devout man … well spoken of by all the Jews… 13 … standing by me said to me, 'Brother Saul, receive your sight.' And in that very hour I received my sight and saw him. 14 'The God of our fathers appointed you to know his will, to see the Just One and to hear a voice from his mouth; 15 for you will be a witness for him to all men of what you have seen and heard. 16 And now why do you wait? Rise and be baptized, and wash away your sins, calling on his name.'

THE BIBLICAL ACCOUNTS OF
THE CONVERSION OF SAUL

Acts 26:9–20	Galatians 1:13–24
9 "I myself was convinced that I ought to do many things in opposing the name of Jesus of Nazareth. 10 And I did so in Jerusalem; I not only shut up many of the saints in prison, by authority from the chief priests, but when they were put to death I cast my vote against them. 11 And I punished them often in all the synagogues and tried to make them blaspheme; and in raging fury against them, I persecuted them even in foreign cities.	13 For you have heard of my former life in Judaism, how I persecuted the church of God violently and tried to destroy it; 14 and I advanced in Judaism beyond many of my own age among my people, so extremely zealous was I for the tradition of my fathers.
12 "Thus I journeyed to Damascus with the authority and commission of the chief priests. 13 At midday, O king, I saw on the way a light from heaven, brighter than the sun, shining round me and those who journeyed with me. 14 And when we had all fallen to the ground, I heard a voice saying to me in the Hebrew language, 'Saul, Saul, why do you persecute me? It hurts you to kick against the goads.' 15 And I said, 'Who are you, Lord?' And the Lord said, 'I am Jesus whom you are persecuting. 16 But rise and stand upon your feet; for I have appeared to you for this purpose, to appoint you to serve and bear witness to the things in which you have seen me and to those in which I will appear to you, 17 delivering you from the people and from the Gentiles—to whom I send you 18 to open their eyes, that they may turn from darkness to light and from the power of Satan to God, that they may receive forgiveness of sins and a place among those who are sanctified by faith in me.'	15 But when he who had set me apart before I was born, and had called me through his grace, 16 was pleased to reveal his Son to me, in order that I might preach him among the Gentiles, I did not confer with flesh and blood, 17 nor did I go up to Jerusalem to those who were apostles before me, but I went away into Arabia; and then I returned to Damascus.
19 "Wherefore, O King Agrippa, I was not disobedient to the heavenly vision, 20 but declared first to those at Damascus, then at Jerusalem and throughout all the country of Judea, and also to the Gentiles, that they should repent and turn to God and perform deeds worthy of their repentance.	18 Then after three years I went up to Jerusalem to visit Cephas, and remained with him fifteen days. 19 But I saw none of the other apostles except James the Lord's brother.

The autobiographical account in Galatians is the shortest of the four conversion accounts, and actually was written before the three accounts in Acts. The letter to the Galatians comes from the middle of the 50s AD, and Luke wrote the other three accounts about ten years later. So, put in compositional order, the accounts grow in detail from one to the next. New and interesting aspects of the conversion make themselves known as one goes forward through the testimonies.

Despite their different lengths, the four accounts share the same three–part structure—a prologue, then the narrative of the conversion experience proper, and finally a description of the aftermath.

Part one reflects moral blindness. Saul studied under the best of rabbis, but took his zeal over the line into zealotry. Not satisfied to follow the Torah strictly himself, he took to persecuting those who followed a different interpretation. He arrested Christians, voted for the death penalty, and assisted at their execution. He sent letters to the leaders of foreign synagogues, asking for the arrest of the Christians there. The testimony to King Agrippa indicates that Saul went to more than one foreign country. "I persecuted them even in foreign cities" (Acts 26:11). If the plural there is taken literally then Damascus was not the first of Saul's police actions, nor was it intended to be the last.

Saul's actions do no credit to his religious instincts. He acted "violently" (Galatians 1:13), and "in raging fury" (Acts 26:11), "breathing threats and murder" (Acts 9:1). Do such thoughts and actions belong in the realm of religion? Rather, they reveal a kind of hypocritical moral blindness. Saul was far from mercy, compassion, tolerance, understanding, or empathy, which form the heart of religion. He could see with his eyes, but he was blind in his heart. To such as him Jesus said, "If you were blind, you would have no guilt; but now that you say, 'We see,' your guilt remains" (John 9:41). The Lord Jesus saw that despite Saul's moral blindness, he was capable of great good, and so His grace intervened to convert him—by casting him into physical blindness.

Part two describes physical blindness. Saul and his companions on the journey to Damascus probably belonged to the school of theology that saw a physical disability as a direct punishment from God. During the course of His public ministry, Jesus encountered such Pharisees, some of whom told the man who had been born blind but was healed: "You were born in utter sin" (John 9:34). Even Jesus' own disciples asked Him, "Who sinned, this man or his parents, that he was born blind?" (John 9:2).

For a rabbinical student of this persuasion, to be struck blind himself would mean that God's favor had been withdrawn from him as a consequence of serious sin. To Saul the blindness raised the immediate question, "What sin of mine has caused this misfortune to befall me?" The answer to that question came from the Voice: "Saul, Saul why do you persecute me?" (Acts 9:4). Note, that the Lord did not ask, "Why do you persecute my followers?" but "What do you persecute ME?" Saul's self-righteousness has now been hoisted on the petard of his own theology. His whole ethos has collapsed. No longer the crusading paragon of virtue, he must now construct a whole new worldview.

Saul's companions have fallen from their high horses also (Acts 26:14). Some of them heard the voice without seeing the light (Acts 9:7), while others saw the light without hearing the voice (Acts 22:9). As they lead him by hand into the nearby city of Damascus, all of them are asking the same question: "What did Saul do wrong to deserve this blindness? And do we share in his guilt?" One or the other of them must want to go straight back to Jerusalem and report to the high priest what has happened to his ambassador. At least some of them stay with Saul and are present for his healing, because several days later, Luke records, "his disciples took him by night and let him down over the wall, lowering him in a basket" (Acts 9:25).

Unfortunately, none of our sources have recorded the names of Saul's fellow travelers. Luke, that excellent researcher, may have found some of them and conducted interviews. Whoever they were, Saul's sudden physical blindness challenged their faulty belief system and must have brought about something like a conversion for them as well, the first of many to grow in faith through Saul's experience.

Part three reveals the aftermath. Plenty of evidence demonstrates that the Apostle to the Nations suffered from continuing eye problems throughout the remainder of his life. He thanks the Galatians for standing by him through his illness, and for being willing to give one of their eyes for him, if it had been able to do him good (Galatians 4:15). He writes to the Corinthians that "now we see in a mirror dimly, but then face to face" (1 Corinthians 13:12), and he concludes that same letter (written down by his secretary) by saying that he is adding his signature "in my own hand" (1 Corinthians 16:21).

So the four accounts are not miracle stories, but rather conversion narratives. The physical healing plays a secondary part, but the moral healing is the whole point. Saul does not say, as the old song Amazing Grace says, "I was blind but now I see." Rather, he says, "I persecuted the One whom now I follow."

Galatians and Acts 9 provide somewhat variant accounts of what Saul did in the first years after his conversion. Perhaps the two accounts can be blended in the following way:
* Saul spent several days with the disciples in Damascus (Acts 9:19).
* There was a side trip taken to Arabia (Galatians 1:17).
* Saul returned to Damascus (Galatians 1:17).
* Three years later (Galatians 1:18), sponsored by Barnabas in Jerusalem (Acts 9:27), Saul visited Cephas and James for fifteen days (Galatians 1:18).
* Taken by the brethren to Caesarea, Saul was sent to Tarsus (Acts 9:30), where he remained for a number of years.

In any event, clearly Saul does not begin his missionary work immediately after his conversion. Instead he undergoes a lengthy period of more than a decade of prayer, study, and quiet Christian life. This should be a lesson for those who come to know the Lord Jesus and immediately want to go out and evangelize others. After conversion comes discipleship. Saul must come to know Jesus and His Way in quiet prayer and serious study, conforming his life to the life of Christ. Saul needs to demonstrate that he is a faithful Christian himself, before presuming to convert the nations. While he is taking the time to do that, the Lucan narrative follows the acts of the other apostles, until Saul is ready to take up his own ministry as the apostle Paul (Acts 11:25).

1. What was Christianity called in early times? Acts 9:2, 22:4

2. How did the grace of God operate in the following?

The light	Acts 9:3	
The voice	Acts 9:3–6	
The water of baptism	Acts 9:18, 22:16	
The laying on of hands	Acts 9:17–18	

3. What is demonstrated in the following passages?

Mark 16:17–18	
Acts 9:34, 14:3	
CCC 1507	

4. How did Ananias feel about Saul? Acts 9:10–17

* Have you ever had a bad first impression about someone that God changed around?

5. Find hints of five particular sacraments in the conversion narratives.

Acts 9:18, 22:16	
Acts 9:17, 27	*Confirmation*
Acts 9:19	
Acts 26:18, 20	
Acts 9:17	

6. What "food for the journey of life" does God give to strengthen believers?

Acts 9:19b	
CCC 1324	

* What provides spiritual strength in your life?

7. What did Saul do after his sight was restored? Acts 9:19–22

8. Explain the drama in Acts 9:23–25.

9. How did the disciples in Jerusalem feel about Saul? Acts 9:26

10. What enabled Saul to be accepted by the disciples in Jerusalem? Acts 9:27–29

* Recall a time in your life when someone stood up for you like Barnabas for Saul.

11. Find a recurring plot in these verses.

Acts 9:23–25	
Acts 9:29–30	

12. Who calls whom to conversion?

Acts 22:4–8	
CCC 545	

13. What does God reveal, and in what language does God speak with Saul? Acts 26:14

14. Does God use force to convert Saul? Is force or coercion appropriate for conversion?

Acts 26:13–18	
CCC 160	

15. What type of conversion does Jesus desire, and what does it entail?

Deuteronomy 30:6	
Romans 2:29	
CCC 1430	
CCC 1848	

16. Sin ruptures communion with God and with the church. For this reason, list some things that true conversion requires.

Psalm 51:3–4	
Psalm 51:6	
Psalm 51:10–12	
Acts 22:10	
CCC 1440	
CCC 1490	

17. What is the answer to the question, "What shall I do, Lord?"

When Paul asks it? (Acts 22:10)	
When I ask it?	

18. To whom was Paul sharing his conversion story?

Acts 22:1–16	
Acts 26:1–20	

19. Can you find evidence that after Saul's conversion he spent some time in prayer and discipleship? Galatians 1:15–20

20. Saint Paul shares the story of his dramatic conversion to Christ in Galatians in about how many sentences? Write the story of your own conversion to Christ ten sentences or less. It may not be as dramatic as Saul's but it is yours and it is important.

* Are you willing to share the testimony of how God has worked in your life with others? Pray for opportunities to share about God's mercy and love in your own life.

Chapter 6

Peter and James — AD 43
Acts 10–12

And Peter opened his mouth and said:
"Truly I perceive that God shows no partiality,
but in every nation any one who fears him and does what is right
is acceptable to him.
You know the word which he sent to Israel,
preaching the good news of peace by Jesus Christ (he is Lord of all)."
Acts 10:34–36

Luke has spent the last several chapters narrating the activities of the younger generation of apostles and deacons—Stephen, Philip, John, and Paul. Now, he switches back to describe the actions of the senior apostles, Peter and James. This explains how God fulfilled the prophecy: "Your old men shall dream dreams, and your young men shall see visions" (Joel 2:28, quoted by Peter in Acts 2:17). By now, the younger man Paul has seen a vision, and the older man Peter has dreamt a dream. In both of their lives, the same Spirit has been fruitfully at work.

Five centuries later, Saint Benedict of Nursia (+ AD 547) summarizes the great Christian heritage of respect for both the young and the old: "Samuel and Daniel judged the priests when they were just young boys (1 Samuel 3; Daniel 13). ... So, one who arrives at the monastery at the second hour should realize that he is junior to one who came at the first hour, no matter what his age or status. ... Therefore the juniors should respect their seniors, and the seniors should love their juniors. ... The seniors are to call their juniors by the title 'brother,' but the juniors should call their seniors 'nonnus,' which means 'reverend father.' Whenever the brothers meet one another, the junior should ask a blessing from the senior. When a senior passes by, the junior must rise and give him a place to sit." (*Saint Benedict's Rule,* translated by Terrence G. Kardong [Collegeville, MN: Saint John's, 1996, p. 515].

Luke provides a narrative that is episodic, but not necessarily chronological. The Holy Spirit did not abandon the senior apostles while working with the young and then leave the young to return to their elders. The vision of Paul and the dream of Peter could very well have taken place at the same time, but they had to be recounted in the narrative one after the other. Within each episode, however, Luke pays a great deal of attention to sequence. The story of Peter and Cornelius takes place over a spread of four days, with the mention of precise times of day.

"Peter went up on the housetop to pray, about the sixth hour" (Acts 10:9). Counting from sunrise, not from midnight, the sixth hour means noontime, when the sun stands in its zenith in the sky, and the sundial casts no shadow at all because the rays of the sun come straight down.

The ancient languages have special words for midday—in Hebrew *Tsohar,* in Greek *Mesembria,* and in Latin *Meridies.* But, the New Testament commonly employs the term "the sixth hour."

Devout Jews pray three times daily, the first prayer at sundown, the second prayer at sunrise, and the third prayer at noon, as expressed in the verse,

> "But I call upon God;
>   and the Lord will save me.
>   Evening and morning and at noon
>   I utter my complaint and moan,
>   and he will hear my voice" (Psalm 55:16–17).

At the three prayer times, ancient Jewish practice called for the opening of windows facing Jerusalem, or going outdoors, to direct the prayer towards the House of God. That is why Peter went to the rooftop to pray. Like thousands of others in the same time zone, he said to himself, "Now is *Tsohar,* and we must pray."

Later, Paul will reveal that the vision came to him on the roadside at the same time of day: "As I made my journey and drew near to Damascus, about noon a great light from heaven suddenly shown about me" (Acts 22:6).

So, the Lord God sent a noontime vision to Paul and a noontime dream to Peter. Whether or not these came on the same day is irrelevant, but the fact that they came at the same time of day is highly significant. That was the hour when thousands of people, both Jews and "God-fearing" Gentiles influenced by Judaism, were offering prayers to the Lord. The Lord answered their prayers by calling Peter and Paul to bring together Jews and Gentiles in a more complete communion of fellowship.

"In it were all kinds of animals and reptiles and birds of the air" (Acts 10:12). The heavenly vision, repeated three times to Peter, countermands the Torah of God. In the beginning there was only one divine positive law—uttered precisely. God told Adam and Eve, "You may freely eat of every tree of the garden; but of the tree of the knowledge of good and evil you shall not eat, for in the day that you eat of it you shall die" (Genesis 2:16–17).

Our first parents probably began life as vegetarians. Later, as a consequence of original sin, death entered the world, and the various kinds of animals, birds, and fish found a place on the human table. However, the Mosaic Code imposed upon the Hebrew people a set of complicated restrictions to limit the food source, combinations and methods of preparing, serving, and cleaning up after their meals.

The kosher laws set the Israelites apart from others, giving them a number of clearly hygienic, but also many seemingly pointless, food regulations. Some rabbis said that the only purpose of these laws, like that original law in the garden, was to test their obedience and help set God's people apart from other nations.

Simon Peter knew the dietary law well, since the separation of kosher from un-kosher seafood had been one of his principal duties on the shores of the Sea of Galilee. Jesus once told a parable based on the experience of Peter and the other fishermen: "The kingdom of heaven is like a net which was thrown into the sea and gathered fish of every kind; when it was full, men drew it ashore and sat down and sorted the good into vessels but threw away the bad" (Matthew 13:47–48).

Interestingly, the heavenly vision does not address the issue of seafood, which was a major dietary staple in the Holy Land as in Rome and throughout the Mediterranean basin. The vision came not to replace one kosher law with another, but to inform Peter that he must begin using the power of the keys bestowed on him by Christ. "I will give you the keys of the kingdom of heaven, and whatever you bind on earth shall be bound in heaven, and whatever you loose on earth shall be loosed in heaven" (Matthew 16:19). Peter alone has the authority in the church to end the excommunication of Jews and Gentiles from each other's tables. Jews might on occasion have a Gentile to supper in a kosher home, but they could never accept a return invitation from the Gentiles. Needless to say, that put very serious dampers on the social calendars of both groups. How could they ever become one church community that way? Peter exercised his authority to promote unity.

"And Cornelius said, 'Four days ago, about this hour, I was keeping the ninth hour of prayer in my house'" (Acts 10:30). Why does a Roman soldier keep the Jewish time of prayer in his home? Cornelius is a typical Latin name, and Luke brings home the point: he was "a centurion of what was known as the Italian Cohort, a devout man who feared God with all his household" (Acts 10:1). A centurion was an officer commanding one hundred foot soldiers. This is not the first respectable centurion to appear in the New Testament (Luke 7:2–9; 23:47). He is one of those God-fearing Romans, some of whom had already received the Holy Spirit in Jerusalem on the first Pentecost (Acts 2:10).

Roman soldiers did not serve for life. Top generals received appointment for a term of five years, and legionnaires enlisted for twenty years, with the right to a grant of land on which to start a family after leaving the service. Cornelius would not retire in the Holy Land. Whenever his tour of duty ended, he and his family would return to Rome and become some of the founding members of the local church there.

Peter spends several days eating with them and sharing the faith, though not keeping kosher. Sharing banquets was very important in Roman and Greek society, not so much for the food as for the exchange of ideas and social cohesion. The head of the apostles, by virtue of the authority vested in him by Christ, looses what the Torah had bound in order to bind the fellowship of the church. The first bishop of Rome begins to create his own community. The Romans to whom Paul later writes, and who receive Paul (Acts 28:15) and Peter in their city, no doubt include some of the younger people from the household of Cornelius. The trajectory of the entire book of Acts is from Jerusalem to Rome. At the beginning, Romans are in Jerusalem; at the end, apostles are in Rome.

"Herod the king laid violent hands upon some who belonged to the church. He killed James the brother of John with the sword" (Acts 12:1–2). This murderous king is Herod Agrippa, grandson of the notorious Herod the Great. The apple has not fallen far from the tree. The Herodian family had a close relationship with the Julian dynasty in Rome. Grandfather Herod had been a good friend of Mark Antony and Augustus Caesar. The grandson was friendly with the Emperors Caligula and Claudius, and the latter appointed him to his grandfather's kingdom, where he served only three years.

Luke displays an uncharacteristic interest in the details of Herod Agrippa's death, because it seemed to be a judgment by God on the king's behavior, "because he did not give God the glory" (Acts 12:23). Flavius Josephus narrates the same event, and mentions that the occasion on which the king was stricken was a celebration of the birthday of the Emperor Claudius. Hence, we know that his reign ended in January of the year AD 44, and that the martyrdom of James the son of Zebedee must have taken place the year or so before. The martyrdom of James comes nearly a full decade after the conversion of Saul, but Luke makes them seem closer together than that. The fluid narrative-flow in Acts sometimes dilates and sometimes contracts the time sequences.

The martyrdom of Stephen the deacon had been the first blow to the early church, but now the beheading of James, senior apostle after only Peter himself, sends a shock wave from the top to bottom of the church. Until now, the apostles assumed that Christ would be returning very soon, while they were still alive. Now they realized that they might die before the return of the Lord took place, leaving the church without the living testimony of those who had known the Lord in person.

Until Saint James' death, the apostles were satisfied to preach the Good News by word of mouth, but now the apostles realized that something had to be put on paper for people to read after they were gone. Apparently, Peter had a young scribe by the name of John Mark, to whom he entrusted the task of setting down on paper the preaching of Peter himself about the Lord Jesus. The death of James seems to have been the impetus for work to begin on the Gospel according to Mark, which has a number of Latin words embedded in the text for the help of converts like Cornelius and other Roman believers.

These senior apostles, Saint Peter, the bishop of the church in Rome and head of the Church, and Saint James the leader of the church in Jerusalem, laid a foundation for the unity and universality of the Church that has remained for two millennia. Catholics today stand on the common profession of faith of Saint Peter and Saint James, senior apostles and followers of Jesus Christ, who each gave their lives in martyrdom for the truth of this Catholic faith. They professed their faith and loyalty to Jesus Christ, and offered their lives in the sure hope of the resurrection of the dead, and an eternity of bliss in His presence in heaven.

The Chair of Saint Peter

Peter expressed in the first place, in the name of the apostles, the profession of faith: "You are the Christ, the son of the living God" (Matthew 16:16). This is the task of all the successors of Peter: to be the leader in the profession of faith in Christ, the Son of the living God. The chair of Rome is, first of all, the chair of this creed. From the loftiness of this chair, the Bishop of Rome is obliged to repeat constantly *"Dominus Iesus,* (Jesus is Lord)." ... The chair of Peter obliges its incumbents to say, as Peter did at a moment of crisis of the disciples, when they wished to go away: "Lord, to whom shall we go? You have the words of eternal life; and we have believed, and have come to know, that you are the Holy One of God" (John 6:68–69). Whoever sits on the chair of Peter must remember the words that the Lord said to Simon Peter at the Last Supper: "And when you have returned again, strengthen your brethren" (Luke 22:32). The holder of the Petrine ministry must be conscious of being a frail and weak man, as his own strength is frail and weak, constantly needing purification and conversion. But, he can also be conscious that from the Lord he receives strength to confirm his brethren in the faith and to keep them united in the confession of Christ, crucified and Risen.

Pope Benedict XVI, *General Audience* (May 7, 2005)

1. Explain some things about Cornelius from the passages below.

Acts 10:1–2	
Acts 10:3–4	
Acts 10:5–8	
Acts 10:22–23	
Acts 10:31	
Acts 10:44–49	

2. What can you recall about Peter from the Gospels?

Matthew 4:17–20	
Matthew 10:2	
Mark 5:36–41	
Mark 9:2–8	
Luke 5:1–11	
Matthew 14:28–33	
Matthew 16:16–18	
Luke 22:31	
John 20:2–9	
John 21:7, 15–19	

3. In your own words, explain Peter's vision. Acts 10:9–16

4. What happened following Peter's vision? Acts 10:17–33

5. What did Peter say to Cornelius and his household? Acts 10:34–43

6. Explain the significance of the following verses, using the Catechism.

Acts 10:41	
CCC 995	
Acts 10:42	
CCC 679	
Acts 10:48	
CCC 1226	

7. What followed Peter's preaching? Acts 10:44–49

8. How did Peter see himself?

Acts 10:26	
1 Peter 5:1–2	
2 Peter 1:1	

9. How did Jesus see Peter? How should you see Peter and his successors?

Matthew 16:17	
CCC 552	
CCC 553	
CCC 881	

10. Who is the successor of Peter, the living authority of Christ on earth today?

CCC 882	
CCC 891	
CCC 892	

* Why do you think it is important to have a living church authority on earth?

* Find or write your own prayer for the Holy Father.

11. How did the disciples react to Peter's involvement with Cornelius? Acts 11:1–3

12. How did Peter respond to his accusers? Acts 11:4–17

13. What significance does the Church place on households?

Acts 11:14	
CCC 1655	

14. Where did the disciples of Jesus Christ first receive their name? Acts 11:19–26

15. Describe Peter's adventure in Acts 12:1–19.

16. Explain the behavior of a woman disciple in Acts 12:12–15

* How do you think you would act in a time of Christian persecution?

17. Who was the first apostle to be martyred? Acts 12:2

18. What can you learn about the Saint James mentioned in Acts 12:2?

Mark 1:19–20	*Fisherman, son of Zebedee, brother of John*
Mark 3:16–17	
Mark 5:35–41	
Mark 9:2–8	
Matthew 20:20–28	
Mark 14:32–34	
Luke 9:54–56	

19. Another James is mentioned in Acts 12:17. List some facts about this James.

Mark 3:18	*James, son of Alphaeus*
Mark 2:14	*Levi (Matthew) is also a son of Alphaeus, brothers?*
Acts 15:13–33	
Acts 21:15–19	
Galatians 1:19	

20. How does the author of The Letter of James describe himself? James 1:1

Chapter 7

Paul and Barnabas — AD 47
Acts 13–14

**While they were worshiping the Lord and fasting,
the Holy Spirit said,
"Set apart for me Barnabas and Saul
for the work to which I have called them."**
Acts 13:2

For fifteen years, from the first Pentecost to the martyrdom of James, the incipient Christian movement functioned within the bosom of larger Judaism. The movement expressed an early interest in the Samaritans, and in the Gentile God-fearers, but that interest did not constitute a break with Judaism in and of itself. The conversion of Saul neutralized the most violent opposition to Christianity and gave the church an extra decade or so to continue for all practical purposes as a Jewish movement. Every spring, pilgrims would arrive in Jerusalem to fulfill their Jewish duties and would be exposed to the preaching of the apostles. Some would return as Christians to their own country and encourage others to come. So, for a decade and a half, Jerusalem was the home base for the followers of Christ.

The martyrdom of James signaled a warning to the Christians, by now spread to every country that it might not be safe to come to Jerusalem any more. The apostles soon noticed a reduction in the number of pilgrims available for evangelization. They realized that Christianity needed a new operational center. While the apostles themselves remained in Jerusalem, they sent representatives to the community in Antioch to encourage that city to become a new missionary base.

Antioch was a logical choice, since it was a great center of Greek culture and learning in the region, founded by Seleucus, a general of Alexander the Great. The third largest city in the Roman Empire, after Alexandria and Rome, Antioch was the capital of the rich province of Syria, and also had a large Jewish population. The Antiochene suburb of Daphne was almost entirely Jewish. Because of the proximity to the Holy Land, a high percentage of the Antiochene Jews had made pilgrimage to Jerusalem. Nearly all of them passed through the customs post at Capernaum, where they might have met a young tax collector named Matthew, who later wrote his gospel in Antioch. Some of the Antiochenes may have heard the Sermon on the Mount (Matthew 4:24ff). One of the first seven deacons, Nicolaus, was a proselyte from Antioch (Acts 6:5). So the church had links to Antioch already and reached out in that direction in the wake of James' martyrdom.

"Now in the church at Antioch there were prophets and teachers" (Acts 13:1). With these words, Luke provides a glimpse into the governing structure of the early Christian community there. Whereas the Jerusalem church has twelve apostles and seven deacons, the Antiochene church has five notable teachers:

— Joseph, called Barnabas, a Levite from Cyprus (Acts 4:36)
— Simeon, called Niger
— Lucius of Cyrene
— Manaen from the court of Herod the tetrarch
— Saul of Tarsus.

Barnabas seems to be the senior elder, and Saul the junior in this list. The two of them have been connected, however since the very time of Saul's conversion, when "Barnabas took him, and brought him to the apostles, and declared to them how on the road he had seen the Lord" (Acts 9:27).

Ten years later, the apostles send Barnabas to Antioch to witness the progress the local church there has made, and Barnabas functions as a kind of legate from the Jerusalem leaders. Barnabas functions as the ambassador of Peter to Antioch, until such time as Peter can go there himself (Galatians 2:9).

Throughout church history, the popes and patriarchs have sent out ambassadors to represent them to the wider Christian world and to foreign governments. The Vatican diplomatic corps is the oldest continuously functioning ambassadorial service in the world, going back to the earliest centuries of church history, with an outstanding record of service in the cause of peace and civil harmony. The principal function of the service, though, is to do exactly what Barnabas did—reinforce the bond of unity between the local church communities and the apostolic center.

One of the first ways Barnabas helps the Antiochene church is to go to Tarsus and recruit Saul, who has been in retreat there for a decade or so. They spend a fruitful year teaching together in Antioch, with Saul under the sponsorship of Barnabas. Although there is a council of five, Barnabas and Saul form a mission partnership of elder and youth, like the teaming up of Peter and John earlier in Acts. Antioch is only the beginning, the launching pad for the ministry of Barnabas and of Saul.

"Being sent out by the Holy Spirit, they went down to Seleucia; and from there they sailed to Cyprus" (Acts 13:4). The Holy Spirit initiates and empowers evangelism. On what is called the First Missionary Journey, Barnabas and Saul visit Cyprus and parts of Asia Minor. Cyprus is the familiar home country of Barnabas.

Earlier in Acts, Luke revealed the origins of Barnabas: "Thus Joseph who was surnamed by the apostles Barnabas (which means, Son of encouragement), a Levite, a native of Cyprus, sold a field which belonged to him, and brought the money and laid it at the apostles' feet" (Acts 4:36). When Cypriot Christians went to Antioch preaching to the Greeks as well as the Jews, the apostles sent Barnabas, a fellow Cypriot well known to them, as their legate to Antioch (Acts 11:20–22). Barnabas leads Saul to Cyprus to introduce him to all the people and places he knows there, expanding Saul's knowledge and experience in the field. They cross the whole island of Cyprus, from Salamis in the east to Paphos in the west.

Similarly, Luke takes care to note the provenance of Saul: "Rise and go to the street called Straight, and inquire in the house of Judas for a man of Tarsus named Saul" (Acts 9:11). Since the people of Tarsus had full Roman citizenship, the presence of Saul on the mission team opened doors that might not have been open otherwise. Perhaps Saul was the reason that Barnabas got entry to see the proconsul Sergius Paulus, the chief administrator of the senatorial province of Cyprus.

The dynamics of the second half of the journey, to the provinces of Pisidia and Lycaonia, are not so clear. Either Barnabas or Saul, or both, must have had some prior connection to people of those areas, just as they had contacts in Cyprus already. Perhaps one link is that a city in Pisidia bore the name Antioch, just like their home base in Syria. Both cities had been founded by Alexander's general Seleucus and were Hellenistic centers in the area. The two Antiochs were probably like sister cities, with Greek speakers going back and forth between the two of them. So Saul and Barnabas make an effort to familiarize themselves with both Antiochs, laying the foundation for extended outreach in the region. Saul will visit Antioch of Pisidia again on his third missionary journey.

"Saul, who is also called Paul" (Acts 13:9) — In the midst of the first missionary journey, the younger member of the mission team begins to appear under the name Paul for the very first time. Already he has appeared in the narrative eighteen times under the name Saul, both before and after his conversion. A number of years transpire between his conversion (AD 35), and the beginning of his mission (AD 41), at which time the alternative name Paul begins to appear. Paul is not his baptismal name but his ministerial name.

Many apostles and evangelists have more than one name, a Hebrew name of the covenant, and a Greek or Aramaic name of mission. Jesus gave Simon bar-Jona, head of the apostles, the name "Rock," which is Cephas in Aramaic and Peter in Greek. The apostle called in some places by the Hebrew name Nathanael, appears in other places by the Aramaic/Greek Bartholomew ("Son of Ptolomy"). The apostle Matthew in Aramaic was originally known as Levi in Hebrew. The apostle Jude, in Hebrew, is also known by the Greek name Thaddeus. In every one of these cases, the name of circumcision, of the covenant, is Hebrew, while the name of action and ministry is Greek or Aramaic. In most of these cases, the second name does not replace the first but continues to be used alongside the original name in different contexts, among different communities. Luke wrote, "Saul, who is also called Paul," not that he ceased to be Saul when he became Paul but that he may be known by either or both names.

Barnabas is already using a *"nom de guerre,"* because his Hebrew name is Joseph and the name Barnabas is an Aramaic construction. *Bar* is the Aramaic for "son of," and *Nabya* is Aramaic for "prophet" or according to Luke, "encouragement." Sometimes Paul uses his old name, when reflecting on his earlier life (Acts 22:7; 22:13; and 26:14). The name Saul never appears outside the Acts of the Apostles, even in Paul's own letters.

Where did the name Paul come from? The name first appears after Saul has met the proconsul Sergius Paulus, governor of Cyprus (Acts 13:7). Luke describes him as an intelligent man who sought to hear the word of God and believed, for he was astonished at the teaching of the Lord. Paul gave this high Roman official the gift of membership in the family of God, and in return apparently received the gift of membership in this man's noble family. The Roman aristocracy frequently adopted political allies, friends and freed slaves. Roman emperors sometimes adopted the men whom they wished to succeed them on the throne. So, the proconsul adopting Paul fits into the patterns of Roman nobility.

For Paul the new name meant that many new doors opened to him. From birth he had already been a Roman citizen of the lowest caste, but with the new name he rose to the top of the social ladder, higher than any of the other apostles. Peter could circulate among Jews and lower Roman military officers, but Paul could now move among the highest circles of the Empire.

"Barnabas they called Zeus, and Paul, because he was the chief speaker, they called Hermes" (Acts 14:12). The reaction of the pagan Lystrians reveals their first impressions. Paul is loquacious like the Greek messenger god Hermes (Mercury in Latin), while Barnabas is dignified and stately like the father god Zeus (Jupiter in Latin). Both men knew Greek and Aramaic, but not the local Lycaonian language.

After Acts 15, Barnabas disappears from the pages of the New Testament. Others take his place as traveling companions of Paul, only now Paul becomes the senior. According to tradition, Barnabas met a martyr's death in his home country of Cyprus, and his body was found with his own hand-written copy of the Gospel of Matthew resting over his heart. Since that Gospel was written after the year 70 AD, Barnabas must have outlived Paul. Tertullian in the second century attributes the Letter to the Hebrews to Barnabas. Since Barnabas was a Levite (Acts 4:36) and the Letter to the Hebrews displays Levitical language, Tertullian's assertion has some credibility. Probably Barnabas did not write the "Epistle of Barnabas" dated about 130 AD, but nonetheless this writing displays a sincere effort to capture the spirit of the man, since it conveys an encouraging tone.

> If you will accept my well-meant advice: you have in your community persons to whom you can do good; do not miss your opportunity! The day is at hand when all things will perish together with the Evil One. At hand is the Lord and His recompense. Again and again I exhort you: be your own good lawgivers; remain your own trusty advisers; away with all hypocrisy! May God, who is Lord over the whole world, grant you wisdom, understanding, insight, knowledge of His just demands, and patient endurance. Be learners in God's school, studying what the Lord requires of you; and then do it! Thus you will be approved on Judgment Day. ... I wanted to cheer you. Farewell, children of love and peace! May the Lord of glory and of every grace be with your spirit!
>
> *Ancient Christian Writers: The Didache, Epistle of Barnabas,* translated by James Kleist, (Westminster, MD: Newman Press, 1948), pp. 64–65.

1. How were Paul and Barnabas commissioned for their missionary activity?

Acts 13: 1–3	
CCC 699	

2. In your own words, explain the drama in Acts 13:4–12.

3. What did Paul do on his arrival in Pisidia? Acts 13:13–15

4. Who did Paul speak to in the synagogue? Acts 13:15–16

5. Summarize the main points of Paul's speech. Acts 13:17–39

6. Were some people able to keep the law perfectly or did they need justification?

Acts 13:38–41	
CCC 578	

7. Find the common warning in the following verses.

Habbakuk 1:5	
Acts 13:40–41	

8. How was Paul's speech first received? Acts 13:42–43

9. List and explain some marvels of the Holy Spirit described by Luke.

Acts 2:1–4	
Acts 3:1–9	
Acts 5:12–16	
Acts 9:36–42	
Acts 13:48–49	
CCC 2640	

10. How did the Gentiles and the Jews respond to the Gospel? Acts 13:48–52

11. Explain the events in Acts 14:1–7.

12. What do signs and wonders demonstrate?

Acts 14:8–11	
CCC 1507	

* Have you ever witnessed a miracle, a sign or a wonder from God? Explain.

13. Could a pagan come to know God or be responsible for seeking God?

Acts 14:15–18	
Romans 1:19–20	
CCC 32	

* How did you come to know about God in your life? Who told you about God?

14. How did Paul see himself and explain himself? Acts 14:15

15. What happened to Paul in Acts 14:19–20?

16. What happened after Paul and Barnabas preached in Derbe? Acts 14:20–21

17. We share in the Lord's Resurrection. What else do we share and why?

Acts 14:22	
CCC 556	
CCC 2847	

18. What did Paul and Barnabas do for the disciples? Acts 14:22a

19. How were Paul and Barnabas commended for their work? Acts 14:26

20. With what were the disciples filled? Acts 13:52

* Barnabas was an encourager. Who encourages you and who can you encourage?

Chapter 8

The Apostles in Council — AD 49
Acts 15

**And after there had been much debate, Peter rose and said to them,
"Brethren, you know that in the early days God made choice among you,
that by my mouth the Gentiles should hear the word of the gospel and believe.
And God who knows the heart bore witness to them,
giving them the Holy Spirit just as he did to us;
and he made no distinction between us and them,
but cleansed their hearts by faith.
Now therefore why do you make trial of God by putting a yoke upon the neck
of the disciples which neither our fathers nor we have been able to bear?
But we believe that we shall be saved through the grace of the Lord Jesus,
just as they will."**
Acts 15:7–11

During the first years of the church, when all the apostles were permanently residing in Jerusalem, the twelve apostles were in daily consultation with one another, under the leadership of Simon Peter in the power of the Holy Spirit. Before long, the apostles began to fan out on mission journeys like that of Peter and John to Samaria. Still, they returned to their home base in Jerusalem where they continued to give and receive counsel. After the blow of the martyrdom of James, however, the quorum of apostles no longer met in continual session. Agenda began to accumulate requiring the attention of the top leadership, and a formal synod became necessary. The apostles create a conciliar structure, which proves of value to address the immediate needs of that time, but also the coming needs of the church over the course of the millennia.

The apostolic council of AD 49 is the first of many councils in church history, right up to our own time. Under the Pope, the successor of Saint Peter, the local bishops have responsibility for the ordinary pastoral care of God's people. Whenever serious general need arises, however, one option available to the Holy Father is to call a general council of bishops to meet with him. Such a council participates in the charism of infallibility, which inheres in the whole church and the entire body of bishops, when they are in union with the pope and with each other.

About five hundred years ago, the idea of "conciliarism" maintained that the body of bishops had authority over individual bishops including the pope. This notion was recognized as incorrect, because a council without a pope in it would not have the same standing as a council with the pope. Therefore, the presence of the successor of Peter, called "first among equals," in the council, or at least his affirmation of the decrees of the council after the fact, elevates the council deliberations to the level of general Magisterium. There can be no council without the pope, or against the pope, but only with the pope. Luke seems to make this point by showing how Peter was the first to grapple with the issues that would later come before the Council of Jerusalem.

"Then after fourteen years I went up again to Jerusalem with Barnabas, taking Titus along with me. I went up by revelation" (Galatians 2:1–2). A lot has happened during the fourteen years between Paul's conversion and the Council of Jerusalem. Peter himself, with his vision on the eve of his meeting with Cornelius, was at the forefront of the movement outwards to the wider world. The activity of the Antioch church was the spark that occasioned the council, but the background situation had been in the making for a long time. If the church was for all nations, what did other people have to do to enter into communion with the church?

"I laid before them (but privately before those who were of repute) the gospel which I preach among the Gentiles, lest somehow I should be running or had run in vain" (Galatians 2:2). Luke puts it this way: "They declared all that God had done with them" (Acts 15:4). Paul's account in the Letter to the Galatians adds more detail about how the facts of the case were outlined to the council. "But even Titus, who was with me, was not compelled to be circumcised, though he was a Greek" (Galatians 2:3).

Luke is the one who gives extra information that "some believers who belonged to the party of the Pharisees rose up and said, 'It is necessary to circumcise them, and to charge them to keep the law of Moses'" (Acts 15:5). The dispute was over what to do with Titus—should he be circumcised, and thus accept the entire Mosaic law as a condition for membership in the church, or if not, then what should he be required to do?

"They saw that I had been entrusted with the gospel to the uncircumcised, just as Peter had been entrusted with the gospel to the circumcised" (Galatians 2:7). Luke's fuller account shows that, after Paul's presentation and the attempted refutation by the Pharisees, Peter spoke, and then James. Peter claims for himself the origins of the Gentile mission: "In the early days God made choice among you, that by my mouth the Gentiles should hear the gospel and believe" (Acts 15:7). Paul in his rhetorical style makes the choice seem either/or—circumcised for Peter, uncircumcised for Paul. In fact, Paul ministered to both groups, as did Peter. The question was one of emphasis or degree. Peter worked mainly with the circumcised, the Jews. Paul preached mainly to the uncircumcised, the Gentiles.

"James and Cephas and John, who were reputed to be pillars, gave to me and Barnabas the right hand of fellowship, that we should go to the Gentiles and they to the circumcised" (Galatians 2:9). James the son of Alphaeus has an important position among the apostles at this time as the first Bishop of Jerusalem. Hence, he is the one who first states and then later writes the conciliar acts. The Acts of the Apostles and letters of the apostles give a window into the life of the early Christian community. The importance of the apostles Peter and James emerges from the order in which they speak at the Council of Jerusalem.

"Only they would have us remember the poor, which very thing I was eager to do" (Galatians 2:10). Paul does not state the conclusions of the council, which required three things of converts—to avoid idolatry, unchastity, and the eating of strangled animals. Rabbis of the time taught that these commandments were given after the flood to Noah for all of the nations. The apostles conclude that Gentile converts must follow the covenant of Noah. The council thus does not abrogate the Torah, which contains the covenants with Noah (for all peoples), Abraham (for many nations), and Moses (for the Jews).

Rabbis at the time of Jesus posed the question, "What do Gentiles need to do to be saved?" They decided that they did not have to convert to Judaism but had to keep only three universal commandments.

1) Avoid idolatry, as embodied in the first commandment, "I am the Lord thy God, thou shall not have strange gods before me." Romans could no longer worship Zeus, nor the Emperor, nor could they eat meat that had been sacrificed to idols.

2) Avoid immorality, as in the sixth commandment, "Thou shall not commit adultery," and also the ninth, "Thou shall not covet thy neighbor's wife."

3) Avoid murder, as in the fifth commandment: "Thou shall not kill." Note that this third ruling seems to differ from the decision of the apostolic Council, which is to avoid the meat of strangled animals. In Kosher practice, the animal's throat is slit, and the carcass is hung to let the blood drain out. Blood is a symbol of life, and not eating bloody meat was an expression of respect for life.

The early rabbis and the early apostles are practically on the same page here. Both pose the question, "What must the Gentiles do?" They come up with practically the same answer. Neither Jews nor Christians can have anything to do with false worship, immorality, or the shedding of innocent blood.

It seemed proper to the Holy Spirit and to us to lay no greater burden upon you than this: It is necessary for you to abstain from meat sacrificed to idols and from blood and from fornication. You will do well to observe these things." The Holy Spirit overlooked many things, but He bound us to these things under pain of capital danger. Other sins are remedied by compensatory works of supererogation; but these crimes are to be feared, for they do not merely weaken the soul but snatch it quite away. Stinginess is redeemed by generosity; insult by apology, harshness by gentleness; amends are made by practice of the opposite ... [But,] what can he do who was contemptuous of God? What shall the murderer do? What remedy shall the fornicator find? These are capital sins, brethren, these are mortal.

Saint Pacian of Barcelona (379–392 AD), *Sermon Exhorting to Penance,*
PL 13, 1081–1090

ECUMENICAL CHURCH COUNCILS

COUNCIL	CONCERNS
Jerusalem AD 49 AD 49	Established the conversion requirements for pagans who want to become Christians.
Nicea 325, Pope Saint Sylvester	Decreed the consubstantiality of the Son of God with the Heavenly Father. Gave the Church the Nicean Creed. Fixed the date for keeping Easter.
Constantinople I 381, Pope Saint Damasus	Defined the consubstantiality of the Holy Spirit, with God the Father, and Jesus the Son.
Ephesus 431, Pope Saint Celestine I	Declared that the Blessed Virgin Mary is the Mother of God (*Theotokos*), in defense of Mary's divine maternity, against Nestorius who claimed that she was only the mother of the man Christ.
Chalcedon 451, Pope Saint Leo the Great	Defined the two natures of Christ, declaring that Jesus is fully human and fully divine.
Constantinople II 553, Pope Vigilius	Condemned the writings of Nestorian heretics, who postulated two separate persons in Christ.
Constantinople III 680–681, Pope Saint Agatho	Defined the two wills in Christ, the divine and the human, as two distinct principles of operation.
Nicea II 787, Pope Adrian I	Condemned iconoclasm, the destruction of holy images.
Constantinople IV 869–870, Pope Adrian II	Defined the *filioque* of the creed, stating that the Holy Spirit proceeds from the Father *and the Son*. Affirmed clerical celibacy.
Lateran II 1123, Pope Callistus II	Dealt with church discipline and the recovery of the Holy Land from infidels.
Lateran II 1139, Pope Innocent II	Enacted reforms suggested by Saint Bernard of Claivaux and preached a crusade against Islam.

Lateran 1179, Pope Alexander III	Condemned Albigenisan and Waldensian heresies and issued decrees for the reformation of morals. Set the requirement for the election of the pope by a two-thirds majority of the voting cardinals.
Lateran IV 1215, Pope Innocent III	Defined transubstantiation—the body and blood, soul and divinity of Our Lord Jesus Christ is really and substantially present in the Holy Eucharist. Revived preaching in Sunday Mass.
Lyons I 1245, Pope Innocent IV	Developed reforms for a lax clergy. Directed a new crusade against the Saracens.
II Lyons 1274, Pope Gregory X	Saint Thomas Aquinas died en route to this council. Saint Bonaventure attended. The dogma of the *filioque* was added to the symbol of Constantinople. Rules for papal elections were laid down.
Vienne 1311–1313, Pope Clement V	Dissolved the Knights Templar. Reformed the clergy, and dealt with the teaching of Oriental languages.
Constance 1414–1418, Pope Martin V	Dealt with the schism of anti-popes in Avignon and attempted to end divisions in the church.
Florence *(Basel)*, 1431–1445, Pope Eugene IV	Decreed that there is no salvation outside of the Church. Tried to bring peace to Christendom.
Lateran V 1512–1517, Pope Leo X	Primarily dealt with disciplinary decrees. Reaffirmed the authority of the pope.
Trent, 1545–1563, Pope Pius IV	Reformed the discipline of the Church. Issued dogmatic decrees on the Holy Eucharist, the Holy Sacrifice of the Mass, and the Sacraments.
Vatican I 1869–1870, Pope Pius IX	Decreed the infallibility of the pope when speaking *ex cathedra*, when as shepherd of the Church, he defines a doctrine concerning faith or morals.
Vatican II 1962–1965, Pope Paul VI	Dealt with liturgy, ecumenism, the Church in the world, lay apostolate, and priestly and religious life.

1. What controversy did the early Church face? Acts 15:1–2

2. How does Paul recount the Council of Jerusalem? Galatians 2:1–9

3. Who did Paul recognize as pillars of the early Church? Galatians 2:7–9

4. Who traveled to the Jerusalem with Paul? Galatians 2:1

5. Find differences in the accounts of the Council of Jerusalem from Luke and Paul.

Acts 15:1–21	Galatians 2:1–9

6. How did people respond to the preaching of the gospel of Jesus? CCC 595

7. How was the controversy over circumcision discussed? Acts 15:2, 7

8. What is the significance of the first person to address the council after debate?

Acts 15:7	
Matthew 16:18–19	
Luke 22:31	

9. How did he address the elders, and what was his argument? Acts 15:7–11

10. How did the assembly respond to Peter's words? Acts 15:12

11. What can you learn about keeping the Mosaic Law perfectly?

Acts 15:10	
Matthew 5:17–19	
John 7:19	
Galatians 5:2–3	
James 2:10	
CCC 578	

12. Who gave the concluding address at the Council of Jerusalem? Acts 15:13

13. What do the words of the prophets affirm?

Isaiah 45:21–22	
Amos 9:11–12	
Acts 15:13–18	

14. What three things were Gentile converts required to do? Acts 15:19–21

15. Explain the decision recounted in Acts 15:22–28.

16. What was sent, and how did the people respond in Acts 15:30–31?

17. What did Judas and Silas do?

* Describe a time when you were exhorted or strengthened. What was the result?

18. Who set off on missionary journeys? Acts 15:36–41

19. What happened in Acts 15:39?

* Have you ever been involved in a contentious situation that turned out well?

20. Select three Church Councils that you find most interesting and explain.

Monthly Social Activity

This month, your small group will meet for coffee, tea, or a simple breakfast, lunch, or dessert in someone's home. Pray for this social event and for the host or hostess. Try, if at all possible, to attend.

After a short prayer and some time for small talk, write a few sentences about "someone who was, or is, an encourager" to you. Then write another sentence about how God enables you to encourage someone else. Try to share about each of these situations in a five-minute time frame.

Examples

◆ *My grandmother encouraged me to practice the piano, and she always asked me to play for her, and complimented my performance.*

◆ *My teacher in high school encouraged me to pursue an occupation in which I could work with my hands, because he noticed how skillful I was at making things in class.*

◆ *I was able to encourage my nephew to continue with his studies, even though he was very discouraged at the time.*

Chapter 9

Paul and Silas — AD 50
Acts 15:36–16:40

**Believe in the Lord Jesus, and you will be saved,
you and your household.**
Acts 16:31

In the year 50, exactly halfway through the First Century AD, the situation in Jerusalem continued to deteriorate. In March, as crowds were swelling in the days leading up to the Passover, a soldier in the Temple precincts bared his posterior to the crowd of worshippers. The larger outer courtyard, the Court of the Gentiles, was surrounded by a colonnade. The military had watch posts atop the colonnade from which they could observe the crowd below. Doors led out from the second story of the adjacent Antonia Fortress to allow the soldiers to take up their posts without having to mingle with the crowd. From this safe perch up on the balustrade, a Roman soldier succumbed to the temptation to express his contempt for the crowd.

Josephus the historian tells how a riot and panic broke out among the outraged Jews and God-fearers below, and how a large number of people were trampled to death. Jewish zealots sought revenge on the military by waylaying the imperial legate Stephanus in the countryside and robbing him. The Prefect Cumanus ordered the surrounding villages pillaged, during which a Book of the Law was desecrated. From outrage to outrage, matters kept getting worse and worse, until the Prefect ordered the sacrilegious soldier to be beheaded. Things then calmed down, but remained tense.

Naturally in an atmosphere such as this, Jews and Jewish Christians alike sent smaller delegations to Jerusalem for the holydays, and many people delayed their lifelong dream of pilgrimage. The apostles in Jerusalem found themselves stranded in an out-of-the-way city, instead of the previously bustling hub of pilgrimage it had been until now. A second missionary journey thus became necessary for Barnabas and Paul, to bring news and especially the letter from the apostles in Council back to the places they had already evangelized, as well as to new places they had never been before.

"And there rose a sharp contention" (Acts 15:39). Paul and Barnabas had been close co-workers. Barnabas was the one who had brought Paul to Jerusalem and introduced him to the apostles. Barnabas went to Tarsus to recruit Paul and bring him back to Antioch, where they had served together as part of the ruling council of five. Barnabas and Paul had gone on the first missionary journey together to Barnabas' country in Cyprus and Paul's country in Asia Minor. The two of them had traveled together to Jerusalem to request the convening of the council of apostles. Yet now, sadly, contention arose between them.

Why did Paul not want John Mark to accompany them, which was seemingly the bone of contention? In later years Mark and Paul will work well together, and will even spend time together in prison. Paul describes Mark as one of his "fellow workers" (Philemon 24) and later as "very useful in serving me" (2 Timothy 4:11). Apparently, then, the controversy arose not from Mark's personality or merits, but as a result of extraneous circumstances. Two possible reasons suggest themselves:

— Peter had a close relationship with the family of John Mark, and went first to their house when the angel released him from prison (Acts 12:12). Perhaps Paul was suspicious of Mark as an observer sent to check up on their preaching. Paul himself mentions that, at the Council of Jerusalem, "false brethren … slipped in to spy out our freedom which we have in Christ Jesus" (Galatians 2:4). Indeed, not all of the leaders had complete confidence in Paul, and they were right to be prudent, in view of the big change Paul had made from persecutor to evangelizer. How could they be sure he would not change again? Paul defends the grace of God which transformed him, and refuses to brook any doubts on the subject.

— Paul reveals that John Mark was a relative of Barnabas (Colossians 4:10). The Greek word he uses, *anepsios*, means "cousin." Luke says that John Mark's mother Mary had a house in Jerusalem (Acts 12:12). Some have suggested that Mary was Barnabas' sister, and that the exact relationship between Barnabas and Mark was that of uncle and nephew. Paul may have objected to Mark's accompanying them because he wanted the mission to be all business rather than a family outing. Nepotism, favoring relatives, has been a corrupting force throughout history. Whatever the reason, the second missionary journey splits the team. Barnabas takes John Mark to his home island of Cyprus, while Paul takes the newcomer Silas to his home country on the mainland of Asia Minor, and on to Europe.

"He took him and circumcised him" (Acts 16:3). At the Council of Jerusalem, Paul deemed it a great victory when the apostles did not require Titus, a Greek convert, to be circumcised. By contrast, Paul circumcises the young Timothy, whose mother was Jewish. According to the law, the child of a Jewish mother is Jewish. So, Paul at this point makes a distinction between Jewish and non-Jewish converts. He requires the Jewish Timothy to submit to circumcision but does not require non-Jews to submit to the law of circumcision.

Paul will maintain a lifelong association with both Timothy and Titus, and later will write to both of them letters that will be accepted into the New Testament canon. Timothy will also accompany him for more than one journey and will be associated with the writing of some of Paul's letters to the churches. Titus is a Latin name, unfortunately the name of the general who will destroy Jerusalem and later become emperor of Rome. Timothy's Greek name means "God-fearer."

"The Spirit of Jesus did not allow them" (Acts 16:7). The whole second missionary journey takes place by the seat of the pants. At every step along the way, God alters the itinerary. Some pilgrims require their trip to be planned down to the last detail. Others travel intuitively, going from place to place by instinct or whim. Paul seems to have found in Silas a person like himself, open to the promptings of the Holy Spirit. Thrown together by the conflict with Barnabas, they now proceed, excluded from Asia by the Holy Spirit, and not allowed by the Spirit of Jesus to enter Bithynia. When doors close, they do not despair but continue on. Expected doors close, but unexpected doors open. In this way, Paul and Silas become the first missionaries to enter Europe. In response to a dream, they sail from Troas on the coast of Asia Minor to the island of Samothrace "and from there to Philippi, the leading city of the district of Macedonia and a Roman colony" (Acts 16:12).

Paul himself is a Roman citizen, and his new name associates him with an important patrician clan in Rome. When he arrives in Philippi and announces, "I am Paul of Tarsus," the local people who are Roman citizens themselves will say, "Welcome, citizen!" When Paul preaches to them, he can say words like those that Shakespeare put into the mouth of Mark Antony in the funeral oration for Julius Caesar: "Friends, Romans, countrymen! Lend me your ears."

"One who heard us" (Acts 16:14). The first person plural appears for the first time in the voice of the narrator of the Acts of the Apostles. Luke seems to indicate that he himself has arrived in Philippi with Paul and Silas. Maybe he joined the group back in Derbe, Lystra, Phrygia, Galatia, or Troas. One clue can be found in the expression that Paul uses later, calling Luke "the beloved physician" (Colossians 4:14). An important shrine of the healing god Askelpios was located at Pergamon, and medical professionals of the day congregated there to share anecdotal information about treatments and cures. Paul later thanks the Galatians for the kindness to him during his illness, and perhaps he met his physician Luke there, and invited him along on the journey. Luke will become Paul's faithful companion, following him to prison (Philemon 23–24), and being Paul's lone companion at the time of his Second Letter to Timothy: "Only Luke is with me" (2 Timothy 4:11).

Luke narrates the meeting with Lydia on the riverside before the meeting with the possessed girl. Actually, the two meetings happened in reverse order. On the way to the river, the slave girl met Paul and shouted, "These men are servants of the Most High God, who proclaim to you the way of salvation!" (Acts 16:17). So, the prophetess may have been instrumental in the conversion of Lydia, who then beseeches Paul and Silas (and Luke) to stay at her house.

Paul gets himself into trouble (again), when he tires of the prophetess and casts out her demons. The slave girl herself profited nothing from her prophetic abilities, but her owners made money off her and now bring charges against Paul. Many people had become dependent upon the prophecies, for guidance in their business dealings and their personal lives. Outraged, they storm the court proceedings and turn them into a riot. The presiding magistrates undoubtedly would have been deferential to Paul, a citizen with a patrician name. But, when the situation gets out of control, they tear off their judicial robes, indicating that the court is adjourned. A kangaroo court follows and not an official Roman court proceeding.

"Suddenly, there was a great earthquake" (Acts 16:26). The whole Aegean area is geologically unstable. About 1630 BC, the island Thera (Santorini) exploded volcanically and spewed ash into the stratosphere, circling the planet, and changing weather patterns for several years. The destruction of Paul's prison matches the description of earthquakes in the area in more recent times. On July 26, 1963, an earthquake measuring 6.1 on the Richter scale hit the Macedonian city of Skopje, destroying one third of the buildings, injuring 4,000 people, and killing 1,300. To the pagans of Paul's time, an earthquake would signify the anger of the gods. Since they had just rioted against Paul and Silas, many would have concluded, "We have incurred the wrath of the gods for our treatment of these men."

The jailer intends to commit suicide because he thinks the prisoners have escaped, but even more because he fears they may have been gods in disguise. Already on the first journey Paul had been mistaken for the god Hermes, the messenger god, and Barnabas had been mistaken for Zeus, the father god. Greek mythology was rife with tales of gods who had assumed human shape in order to walk about the earth, punishing people who treated them rudely.

Paul takes no care for his own freedom, but he liberates his jailer from his false theology and his false sense of honor. Paul tells the jailer not to take his own life, liberating him just as he had liberated the slave girl from her demons. Paul came to a Roman city that proudly thought itself free and, by the power of Christ, he offered liberation from sin and death to that very city. Some, like the slave owners, were unwilling to accept the freedom he offered, but others, like Lydia and the jailer, cast off the invisible chains that bound them.

"Trembling with fear he fell down before Paul and Silas" (Acts 16:29). The proud man bows down before the humble one; the power of humility triumphs over the spirit of pride. Roles are reversed, and in the wake of God's earthquake, everything is turned upside down. Paul does not want to become a new power in his own right. However, he introduces the jailer to the real power in the universe in this world and the next: "Believe in the Lord Jesus, and you will be saved, you and your household" (Acts 16:31). Paul, Silas, Timothy, and Luke teach him the source of supernatural power: "the name which is above every name, that at the name of Jesus every knee should bow, in heaven and on earth and under the earth, and every tongue confess that Jesus Christ is Lord, to the glory of God the Father" (Philippians 2:9–11).

About eight years later, Paul will return to Philippi to celebrate Passover with his Christian community there, and again he will probably stay with his hostess, Lydia, the fabric merchant. Some time before then, Paul and Timothy will write an inspiring letter back to the Christians of Philippi, including the former jailer and his family. Paul will look back on the visit to Philippi as a turning point in his ministry, the first outreach to Europe in the history of the church. Whatever the church has built in Europe, Paul began in the Name of Jesus. He liberated the slave girl in the Name of Jesus and he liberated the jailer by the power of Jesus. True liberation comes through the Redemption won by Jesus Christ for all of humanity.

1. What prompted the decision for Paul and Barnabas to separate? Acts 15:36–39

* Describe some ways in which a disagreement could bear good fruit in ministry.

2. Explain everything you can learn about Timothy.

Acts 16:1–3	
2 Timothy 1:5	
Philippians 2:20–22	

3. Surprisingly, what did Paul ask of Timothy and why?

Acts 16:3	
CCC 527	

4. What did Paul and Timothy do, and with what result? Acts 16:4–5

5. What prompted Paul to go to Macedonia? Acts 16:6–12

6. Who was Paul evangelizing on the sabbath? Acts 16:13–15

7. What is required for baptism, and who may be baptized?

Acts 2:38	
CCC 1226	
CCC 1252	

8. Who was baptized in Acts 16:14–15?

9. Describe the drama in Acts 16:16–22.

10. How can disciples perform miracles and cast out demons?

Acts 16:18	
CCC 434	

11. How did Paul get into trouble in Philippi? Acts 16:18–22

12. What happened to Paul after he liberated the slave girl? Acts 16:22–24

13. How did Paul and Silas spend their time in prison? Acts 16:25

14. Who else faced adversity with faith and joy? Daniel 3:24–45

* Have you ever met someone who faced difficulties by "dancing in the flames?"

15. What happened at midnight? Acts 16:25–26

16. How did the natural disaster affect the prisoners? Acts 16:26

17. Describe the jailer's response. Acts 16:27, 29

18. What did Paul do for the jailer? Acts 16:28, 31

19. What constitutes the "domestic church?"

Acts 16:33–34	
CCC 1655	

20. How does the drama in Acts 16 conclude? Acts 16:35–40

Chapter 10

Philippians — AD 50
Philippians 1–4

**And I am sure that he who began a good work in you
will bring it to completion at the day of Jesus Christ.**
Philippians 1:6

The city of Philippi, located in present-day northern Greece, was situated on a hill in eastern Macedonia. Travelers from Asia Minor to Greece proceeded along the Via Egnatia, the Roman road running from east to west, bringing trade and commerce through the region. Philippi was named after the father of Alexander the Great, Philip II of Macedon, who built a camp in this area in 357 BC. After the battle of Philippi in 42 BC, veterans settled there, bringing Roman citizenship.

Paul had a vision of a man inviting him to come to Macedonia (Acts 16:9). In obedience to God, Paul, Timothy, and Silas arrived in Philippi in AD 50, and there established their first Christian community in Europe (Acts 16:12–40). In Philippi, Paul delivered a slave girl from a demon and ended up in prison. However, an earthquake freed Paul from that prison. Faithful women served the church in Philippi, including Lydia, Euodia, and Syntyche (Acts 16:14, Philippians 4:2). His warm, personal tone reveals a close relationship with the people of Philippi, whom he also visited in AD 57 and AD 58.

Most scholars believe that Saint Paul is the author of the Letter to the Philippians, although it may have been one letter or a compilation of letters. Several references indicate that Paul is writing this letter while in captivity (Philippians 1:7, 13, 14, 17). While it is certain that Paul was writing from prison, it is unclear where he is imprisoned. Philippians may have been written from Caesarea (Acts 23:23ff), or Rome (Acts 28:16–31), or possibly even Ephesus. If written from Ephesus, the letter could be dated as early as AD 54. If written while Paul was imprisoned in Rome, the letter could possibly have been written as late as AD 63.

"To all the saints in Christ Jesus who are at Philippi, with the bishops and deacons" (Philippians 1:1) — Paul and Timothy identify themselves as servants of Christ Jesus and address the Christians of Philippi as saints in Christ Jesus. Living souls can be called *saints*, because of the sanctifying grace received in baptism, even though complete sanctification has not yet been perfected in the believer. Paul gives an early acknowledgement of the roles of bishops and deacons in the church. He then offers thanksgiving and prayer for his friends, who are partners with him in the gospel. Confidently, Paul asserts that he is sure that Jesus Christ will complete the good work that He began in them. And then, Paul gives the Philippians a key to sanctification and growth in holiness. He provides practical, understandable tools for growth in Christian maturity.

"And it is my prayer that your love may abound more and more, with knowledge and all discernment, so that you may approve what is excellent, and may be pure and blameless for the day of Christ, filled with the fruits of righteousness which come through Jesus Christ, to the glory and praise of God" (Philippians 1:9–11).

Love, knowledge, and discernment are essential for growth in holiness. Jesus commanded His disciples to love one another even as Jesus had loved them (John 15:12). Christians must grow in the knowledge of God. They must study the ways of God, and the Word of God, in order to discern what is good from what is evil.

Paul's life is no longer his own but is given over totally to Christ. Through baptism, Paul has died to his old self and is a new creation. Whether he lives or dies, Christ will be glorified, and the truth of the gospel will be advanced. Paul's greatest desire is to be with Christ.

The crowning glory of Philippians is found in the Christocentric hymn in Philippians 2:6–11 that may be original to Paul or may have been an early Christian hymn, possibly composed originally in Aramaic, and inserted here. The hymn appears to have six strophes or stanzas, each containing three lines.

Christ, God's holy servant
Divine Office Canticle — First Vespers of Sunday

Though he was in the form of God,
Jesus did not deem equality with God
something to be grasped at.

Rather, he emptied himself
and took the form of a slave,
being born in the likeness of men.

He was known to be of human estate,
and it was thus that he humbled himself,
obediently accepting even death, death on a cross!

Because of this, God highly exalted him
and bestowed on him the name
above every other name,

So that at Jesus' name
every knee must bend
in the heavens, on the earth, and under the earth,

and every tongue proclaim
to the glory of God the Father:
JESUS CHRIST IS LORD!

Whatever its origin, the Holy Spirit has divinely inspired the human author to place this beautiful hymn here in this place, and the church would be poorer without it. Throughout the Christian world, bishops, priests, religious, and those lay people who pray the Liturgy of the Hours, or Divine Office, pray the Christ Hymn from Philippians 2:6–11 every Sunday vigil during evening prayer proscribed as the Canticle for Evening Prayer for Sunday I, entitled "Christ, God's holy servant."

Saint Augustine of Hippo used this passage from Philippians to refute the Arian heresy of his time and proclaim that Jesus Christ is true-God and true-man. "This unity of person of Christ Jesus our Lord involves each nature, the divine, of course, and the human, so harmoniously that whatever is named peculiar to the one is imparted also to the other, both the divine to the human, and the human to the divine" (Saint Augustine, AD 418, *Against a Discourse of the Arians, treated in the Corrections 2, 78*).

Saints Athanasius and Saint Gregory of Nyssa used this text to defend the full divinity and humanity of Christ, pointing out the significance of the exaltation of Christ, following the humiliation in His humanity. Saint John Chrysostom dedicated two entire homilies to this very text. And Saint Cyril of Alexandria quoted Philippians 2:6–11 over one hundred times in his writings, recognizing the two distinct natures while defending the unity of the person of Jesus Christ.

The exaltation of Christ by God the Father appears in contrast to the humiliation chosen and accepted by Jesus the Son. Beyond the exaltation of the just, Christ, who placed Himself so totally in submission to the will of the Father, now has unique lordship over the whole universe. "For I am God, and there is no other. By myself I have sworn, from my mouth has gone forth righteousness a word that shall not return: 'To me every knee shall bow, every tongue shall swear'" (Isaiah 45:22b–23). Isaiah prophesies the final eschatological reality in which all of creation will pay Jesus the homage that is due to God and God alone.

The prophet Daniel had envisioned a scene in which One like a Son of man would be presented to the Ancient of Days to be exalted. "And to him was given dominion and glory and kingdom, that all peoples, nations, and languages should serve him; his dominion is an everlasting dominion, which shall not pass away, and his kingdom one that shall not be destroyed" (Daniel 7:14).

Saint Paul uses this beautiful example of Jesus Christ and His humility to encourage the Philippians to strive to grow in the virtue of humility. They are encouraged to be of one mind, to do nothing from selfishness or conceit, and to look to the interests of others (Philippians 2:1–4). They are to model their behavior after the perfect example of Christ. They must strive for perfection. The Christians collectively must work out their salvation in fear and trembling, trusting that God is at work to bring each of them to a reward in heaven. Moreover, they must be blameless and innocent, without blemish (Philippians 2:15). The believers are encouraged to do all things without grumbling or questioning, in contrast to the murmuring and complaining of the Israelites in the desert on their way to the Promised Land (Exodus 16:2).

Despite his captivity, Paul encourages his disciples to "rejoice in the Lord," indeed to "rejoice in the Lord always" (Philippians 3:1, 4:4). Joy is infallible evidence of the presence of God. Paul knows that in this life one can experience pleasure or happiness, but true joy comes from knowing the Lord. Paul prays "that I may *know him* and power of his resurrection, and may share his sufferings, becoming like him in his death, that if possible I may attain the resurrection from the dead" (Philippians 3:10–11). Even though Jesus Christ has ascended to the Father, Paul wants to know Him more and suggests that we can know Him too. The mature Christian moves from *knowing about* the Lord, to *knowing* Jesus as Savior, Lord, and friend. Prayer, listening to God, hearing His Word, and experiencing Him in the sacraments prepare the believer for "our commonwealth [which] is in heaven, and from it we await a Savior, the Lord Jesus Christ, who will change our lowly body to be like his glorious body…" (Philippians 3:20–21).

Apparently there are problems even in the early Christian community, for Paul sees that somehow two co-workers in the Lord, Euodia and Syntyche, have come to a disagreement. He implores the Philippians to help these women to restore their peace. The same encouragement could be offered to the church today, when problems and disagreements threaten to break the unity and harmony of the body. Believers are advised to "have no anxiety about anything, but in prayer and supplication with thanksgiving let your requests be made known to God. And the peace of God, which passes all understanding, will keep your hearts and your minds in Christ Jesus" (Philippians 4:6–7). The fact that Paul experiences peace and joy, while in captivity, gives credence to his words.

Practical wisdom for positive thinking is offered. Negative thinking causes discouragement. Believers should think about what is true, honorable, just, pure, lovely, and gracious. Think about what is excellent and worthy of praise. Following this advice brings good fruit today as it did when it was written centuries ago.

Finally, Saint Paul has learned the virtue of contentment. Whether free or in prison, he has learned to be content. He has known hunger, abundance, and want. Whether in good times or in hard times, Paul has learned to trust God. He has complete trust and confidence in Almighty God, who can do all things and who can strengthen anyone in his need. It would seem to be a normal human emotion for Paul to be discouraged, angry, or depressed. Why was he stuck in confinement when he would rather be out preaching the gospel and starting Christian communities? The Christian community in Philippi no longer exits, but the short letter written while in prison continues to instruct, admonish, and bless believers to this very day, almost 2000 years later.

Complete confidence in God allows Paul to say:

> "And my God will supply every need of yours
> according to his riches in glory in Christ Jesus"
> (Philippians 4:19)

1. Read the Letter to the Philippians and write your favorite verse.

2. How does Paul identify himself and begin this letter? Philippians 1:1–5

3. What confidence does Paul proclaim? Philippians 1:6

4. Describe the emotion Paul has for the Philippians. Philippians 1:7–8

5. What is Paul's prayer? Philippians 1:9–11

6. Describe Paul's present circumstances. Philippians 1:12–15

7. How does Paul see his life? Philippians 1:19–26

8. How could you live a life worthy of the gospel?

Philippians 1:27–2:5	
CCC 1691–1694	
CCC 2842	

* What specific way will you "look to the interests of another" this week?

9. What example or model for living could you choose?

Philippians 2:5–11	
CCC 520	

10. Write your own Hymn to Christ or copy Philippians 2:6–11 on a card.

11. What prompted the early Christians to write hymns? CCC 2641

12. What significance does the name "Jesus" have?

Philippians 2:9–11	
CCC 2666	

13. Find a common behavior discussed in the following verses.

Numbers 16:11–14	
Numbers 21:5–6	
1 Corinthians 10:9–10	
Philippians 2:14–16	

14. What is Paul's attitude and objective? Philippians 3:7–11

15. How does Paul conduct his spiritual life? Philippians 3:12–16

16. Explain Paul's ultimate hope and goal in life. Philippians 3:20–21

17. What directions and promises are given in these verses?

Philippians 4:4	
Philippians 4:6a	
Philippians 4:6b	
Philippians 4:7	

18. What should you focus your mind on? Philippians 4:8

19. What virtue has Paul attained? Philippians 4:11–12

20. How is God expected to meet human needs? Philippians 4:19

* Philippians 4:9 proposes a model for Christian living. What person near to you would you pick as an exemplary model of Christian living? Why?

Chapter 11

Thessalonians — AD 50
Acts 17, 1 and 2 Thessalonians

**The God who made the world and everything in it,
being Lord of heaven and earth, does not live in shrines made by man,
nor is he served by human hands, as though he needed anything,
since he himself gives to all men life and breath and everything
…Yet he is not far from each one of us, for
"In him we live and move and have our being."**
Acts 17:24–25, 27–28

Paul and Silas continue on their second missionary journey, heading overland from Philippi along a major highway to the thriving commercial hub of Thessalonica. The Macedonian general Kassander founded this city around 315 BC and named it after his wife, Alexander's half-sister Thessalonike. The Jewish community there was large enough to have a synagogue.

On the sabbath in Philippi, Paul prayed by the riverside (Acts 16:13), and so the Philippian Jewish community must have been much smaller. Only ten synagogues appear in the Acts— Jerusalem (Acts 6:9), Damascus (Acts 9:2, 20), Salamis (Acts 13:5), Antioch of Pisidia (Acts 13:14, 42), Iconium (Acts 14:1), Thessalonica (Acts 17:1), Beroea (Acts 17:10), Athens (Acts 17:17), Corinth (Acts 18:4), and Ephesus (Acts 18:19). Only two of these synagogues—Antioch of Pisidia and Thessalonica—give Paul a bad reception. Contrast his welcome in Beroea: "Now these Jews were more noble than those in Thessalonica, for they received the word with all eagerness, examining the scriptures daily to see if these things were so" (Acts 17:11). So the general impression that Paul met with rejection in the synagogues is misleading. Most Jewish communities did welcome him.

"For three weeks he argued with them" (Acts 17:2). Paul experienced opposition from pagans in Philippi, but now meets resistance from Jews in Thessalonica. Argumentation was a common method of arriving at the truth in Greek and Jewish public discourse. These communities did not sit back passively and listen to speeches or sermons—they interacted with the presenter by asking questions, raising objections, and sometimes even shouting. Paul was good at this form of argumentation, because he had practiced it from his youth. When some of the Thessalonian Jews argue with Paul, they met their match. The fact that the disputation went on for three weeks means that there was a lot of give-and-take, and not an immediate rejection. Actually, three weeks means three sabbath days, for the Jews met once a week for their worship and theological discussions.

"Jason has received them" (Acts 17:7). During his three weeks in Thessalonica, Paul and his companions stay at the home of a certain Jason, who bears a name well known in the Greek world from the legend of Jason and the Argonauts, who had gone in search of the golden fleece. The name Jason is well attested among diaspora Jews, not as a circumcision name, but perhaps a nickname. Just as Paul became a nickname for Saul, so any Jew named Joshua or Jesse could find in the Greek name Jason a suitable alias. Jason, a Jew from Cyrene wrote a history of the Maccabean revolt, and an abridgement of that work became Second Maccabees.

Jason of Thessalonica may be the same man later mentioned at the end of the Letter to the Romans: "Timothy, my fellow worker, greets you; so do Lucius and Jason and Sosipater, my kinsmen" (Romans 16:21). The Greek word for kinsmen there, *syngenes,* is the same word that the Archangel Gabriel used to describe the relationship between Mary and Elizabeth (Luke 1:36). Sometimes translated cousin or relative, the word literally means "belonging to the same tribe." Luke seems to say that Mary belongs to the same tribe as Elizabeth (daughter of Aaron and member of the tribe of Levi) which would also place Mary in the tribe of Levi. Paul infers that Jason belongs to the same tribe as himself (a Benjamite). Benjamin is the smallest of the twelve tribes. So a traveling Benjaminite would likely seek shelter with a fellow member of the same tribe.

On Paul's first sabbath in the city, his kinsman Jason introduces him to the congregation. Paul gives a message of consolation in the current time of troubles, with the promise of a doctrinal teaching the following week. Paul later writes back to these people and reminds them, "You are witnesses, and God also, how holy and righteous and blameless was our behavior to you believers; for you know how, like a father with his children, we exhorted each one of you and encouraged you and charged you to lead a life worthy of God, who calls you into his own kingdom and glory" (1 Thessalonians 2:10–12). Paul's introductory message on his first sabbath may have been something like his later words: "Encourage one another and build one another up, just as you are doing. ... Be at peace among yourselves. Admonish the idlers, encourage the fainthearted, help the weak, be patient with them all. See that none of you repays evil for evil, but always seek to do good to one another and to all. Rejoice always, pray constantly, give thanks in all circumstances ... abstain from every form of evil" (1 Thessalonians 5:11–22).

On his second sabbath in Thessalonica, Paul gives his major presentation. "He argued from the scriptures, explaining and proving that it was necessary for the Christ to suffer and to rise from the dead, and saying, 'This Jesus, whom I proclaim to you, is the Christ'" (Acts 17:2–3). Jesus Christ dead and risen is the heart of Paul's message everywhere. His letters to Thessalonica reiterate this Christological doctrine: "For God has not destined us for wrath, but to obtain salvation through our Lord Jesus Christ, who died for us so that whether we wake or sleep we might live with him" (1 Thessalonians 5:9–10). Some are convinced, but others go home to ponder the matter.

On his third sabbath, Paul advances from the teaching of Christ's first coming to the topic of the Second Coming of Christ: "When the Lord Jesus is revealed from heaven with his mighty angels in flaming fire, inflicting vengeance upon those who do not know God and upon those who do not obey the gospel of our Lord Jesus. They shall suffer the punishment of eternal destruction and exclusion from the presence of the Lord and from the glory of his might, when he comes on that day to be glorified in his saints, and to be marveled at in all who have believed, because our testimony to you was believed" (2 Thessalonians 1:7–10). This heavy message connects acceptance of Paul's message to the promise of eternal happiness. This requires a leap of faith that many in the congregation simply cannot make.

When Paul taught that Jesus of Nazareth had come as the Messiah, he merely made specific a general doctrine that most Jews of the time already accepted. The idea of a Second Coming in glory, however, seems to constitute a greater challenge to his first listeners. Christ's first coming was in human form; His Second Coming will be in divine form. The stumbling block for the Thessalonians seems to be the divine nature of Christ, though the matter was not presented to them exactly in that form.

Paul's first letters emphasize the doctrine of the Second Coming of Jesus Christ, which seems to form one of the major components in the *kerygma* (proclamation) of the early Church. Paul seems to feel, along with the rest of the apostles, that the return of the Lord is just around the corner, happening very soon. This explains the energy of his sense of mission. He wants as many people as possible, both Jews and Greeks, to know the Lord and prepare themselves for His coming. His own sense of urgency grows as he proclaims this message.

"They dragged Jason and some of the brethren before the city authorities" (Acts 17:6). Jason suffers for sponsoring Paul. The non-Jewish people of the city have him arrested and thrown into prison, but the magistrates release Jason on bond (Acts 17:9). Paul has already slipped safely out of the city but remains concerned for the welfare of Jason and the others. From Athens, he sends Timothy back to check up on the situation (1 Thessalonians 3:2). Paul honors Jason and his fellow Thessalonians for having suffered for the sake of the truth: "And you became imitators of us and of the Lord, for you received the word in much affliction, with joy inspired by the Holy Spirit; so that you became an example to all the believers in Macedonia and in Achaia. For not only has the word of the Lord sounded forth from you in Macedonia and Achaia, but your faith in God has gone forth everywhere, so that we need not say anything" (1 Thessalonians 1:6–8).

"We will hear you again about this" (Acts 17:32). Paul delivers one of his best and clearest teachings in Athens, connecting the God of the Hebrews to the unknown god who was honored in the Athenian cult. Athens, the city of Sophocles, Plato, and Aristotle, was still the major philosophical center of the Mediterranean world. In his writings, Paul seems generally aligned with the Stoic School of Greek philosophy. He knows how to reason in such a way that the Athenians will follow him but, when he reaches the idea of the resurrection, they protest: "Now when they heard of the resurrection of the dead, some mocked; but others said, 'We will hear you again about this'" (Acts 17:32). These Athenians seem to be Platonists, who believe that the material universe is insignificant, while what really matters is the world of ideas. Death to them meant liberation, and return from death would be a return to a lesser plane of existence. The Sadducees were under the influence of Greek ideas, and for that reason, they did not share the belief of other Jews in a final resurrection on the last day. As a Pharisee, Paul already believed in the general resurrection even before his conversion. It is a short step from there to believing that Jesus has already risen. The Greeks had a much larger step to take, since the material body to them was merely an incidental, temporary plane of existence.

Despite his great eloquence, Paul converts hardly anyone in Athens. One of his few converts was Dionysius the Areopagite. Though mentioned nowhere else in the New Testament, Dionysius achieved a kind of legendary status in later centuries, and his name was attached to four liturgical and mystical treatises that appear about the year 500 AD. Because the person whom Paul converted may not have been personally responsible for those writings, they are called "Pseudo-Dionysian."

"After this he left Athens and went to Corinth" (Acts 18:1). There, Timothy returns from Thessalonica and reports that Jason and the others are safe. Paul spends a good deal of time in Corinth, and from there he writes two letters back to the Thessalonians. These are not the first letters Paul has ever written; he again refers to his custom of signing his letters himself at the end of the second letter (2 Thessalonians 3:17). However, they are the first of his letters to be preserved and to enter into the canon of Sacred Scripture. The First Letter to the Thessalonians is the earliest piece of writing in the New Testament, believed to have been written in the Fall of AD 51.

"Paul, Silvanus, and Timothy, To the Church of the Thessalonians" (1 Thessalonians 1:1; 2 Thessalonians 1:1). With these same words both letters begin. These letters are from three people, Paul, Silvanus, and Timothy. The author speaks in the first person plural through the first two chapters of the letter, but then he breaks into first person singular: "We wanted to come to you—I, Paul, again and again—but Satan hindered us" (1 Thessalonians 2:18). He later returns to the first person plural, "But we beseech you, brethren" (1 Thessalonians 5:12). At the very end though, the final words are in Paul's voice alone: "I adjure you by the Lord that this letter be read to all the brethren" (1 Thessalonians 5:27). The second letter again uses the plural throughout, but the singular is even clearer at the end: "I, Paul, write this greeting with my own hand" (2 Thessalonians 3:17).

Paul clearly is the principal author of the letters but he associates Silvanus and Timothy with him. Scholars assume that Silvanus is an alternate version of the name Silas, Paul's principal partner on this missionary journey. Timothy is well known to the Thessalonians. Timothy may be the scribe who writes down the letters and the messenger who carries the letters back to the Thessalonians.

"Before our Lord Jesus at his coming" (1 Thessalonians 2:19)—Here Paul introduces the important word *parousia,* translated "coming." This word occurs nineteen times in the New Testament, and seven of those are within the two letters to the Thessalonians. The prefix *par* means "around" or "about," and the root *ousia* means "being." So, the composite word literally means "being around" or "being present." The doctrine refers not just to the Second Coming of Christ, but that He is returning to stay. He will be really present. The real presence of the Lord in the Blessed Sacrament is thus a true beginning of the *parousia* under the appearance of bread and wine, but the final coming will make Him present in glory.

"Stand firm and hold to the traditions which you were taught by us, either by word of mouth or by letter" (2 Thessalonians 2:15). Paul wants the Thessalonians to have the real thing and so he admonishes them to hold firm to the truth they have received. The Catholic faith stands on three pillars: 1) Sacred Scripture, 2) Apostolic Tradition, and 3) The Teaching Magisterium. These three pillars are not so entirely distinct. Peter and the apostles were the living teachers of their day, and the pope and bishops teach in continuity with the apostolic ministry. The Sacred Scripture is only a partial record of the teachings of the apostles but sufficient to feed the ongoing life of the church.

New questions arose for the apostles in their time and new questions continue to arise for believers in all subsequent times. Therefore, the written record of the apostolic teaching needs to be preached, explained, applied, and theologized by the ruling, teaching, and sanctifying authority that is in our midst.

The Bible is silent on many issues: gambling, artificial insemination, in-vitro fertilization, pornography, and end-of-life dilemmas to name a few. The consistent teachings of the pope and the bishops in union with him give clear direction on how to live a moral Christian life in a way that is pleasing to God.

Catholics believe that everything in the Bible is true. And, when facing a moral dilemma, the Catholic must ask three important questions.
1) What does the Bible say?
2) What was the tradition of the apostles and the early Church?
3) What do the pope and bishops teach about this question?

Jesus said, "You are Peter, and on this rock I will build my church, and the powers of death shall not prevail against it" (Matthew 16:18). Jesus gave us a Church and shepherds, Peter and his successors, the popes. Later, the Church gave us the Bible, not the other way around. First, God gave the Thessalonians an apostle, Paul, and then He gave them two priceless letters that they preserved for us later believers.

> Sacred theology rests on the written word of God, together with sacred tradition, as its primary and perpetual foundation. By scrutinizing in the light of faith all truth stored up in the mystery of Christ, theology is most powerfully strengthened and constantly rejuvenated by that word. For the Sacred Scriptures contain the word of God and since they are inspired really are the word of God; and so the study of the sacred page is, as it were, the soul of sacred theology.
> Second Vatican Council, Dogmatic Constitution *Dei Verbum*, 24 (1965)

1. Identify some main points of Paul's preaching.

Acts 17:2–4	
Acts 17:24–28	
Acts 17:30–31	

2. How did the Beroeans receive the gospel? Acts 17:11

3. How did the Gospel come to the Thessalonians? 1 Thessalonians 1:2–10

4. What is the center of the apostolic faith proclaimed by Paul?

1 Thessalonians 1:9–10	
CCC 442	

5. Describe Paul's ministry in Thessalonica. 1 Thessalonians 2:1–12

6. Explain the significance of the word of God.

1 Thessalonians 2:13–16	
CCC 104	
CCC 105	
CCC 107	
CCC 108	

7. What are the Thessalonians experiencing at this time? 1 Thessalonians 2:14–15

8. How can someone become a co-worker in God's kingdom?

1 Thessalonians 3:1–11	
CCC 307	

* In what ways are you called to be a co-worker in God's kingdom?

9. What does God call each believer to attain? 1 Thessalonians 4:1–8

10. How can you achieve this? CCC 2813

* List two practical ways that you could grow in holiness.

11. What must each Christian do daily?

1 Thessalonians 4:11	
CCC 2427	

12. What hope is found in these passages?

1 Thessalonians 4:13–15	
1 Corinthians 15:51–58 CCC 989	

13. What different things can you learn from these passages?

Matthew 24:4–31	
Mark 13:9–37	
Luke 21:10–28	
1 Thessalonians 4:16–18	
Revelation 20:4–6	
CCC 1001	
CCC 1002	
CCC 1003	

14. How should the Christian then live? 1 Thessalonians 5:1–10

15. List the practical instructions given in 1 Thessalonians 5:11–15

16. How is it possible to obey 1 Thessalonians 5:16–18?

17. How can you tell if something is from God or not? 1 Thessalonians 5:19–22

18. What does 2 Thessalonians 1:5–12 inspire you to do?

2 Thessalonians 1:5–12	
CCC 1041	

19. What can you learn about evil and suffering?

2 Thessalonians 2:1–12	
CCC 385	
CCC 671	

20. Explain the role of Scripture, Tradition, and the Magisterium of the Church.

CCC 81	
2 Thessalonians 2:15	
CCC 82–83	
CCC 85	

* Describe and apply the requests and warnings given in 2 Thessalonians 3.

Chapter 12

The Word to Corinth — AD 51
Acts 18, 1 Corinthians 1–8

Do not be afraid, but speak and do not be silent; for I am with you, and no one shall attack you to harm you; for I have many in this city.
Acts 18:9–10

**Do you not know that your body is a temple of the Holy Spirit within you, which you have from God?
You are not your own; you were bought with a price.
So glorify God in your body.**
1 Corinthians 6:19–20

The eventful second missionary journey continues, as Paul leaves Athens and travels the short distance to the city of Corinth, capital of the province of Achaia (Greece proper), just as Philippi was the capital of the province of Macedonia. Both Philippi and Corinth of New Testament times were Roman colonies, settled by veterans from the imperial legions. The people of those two cities, like those of Tarsus, possessed Roman citizenship. Paul comes among fellow citizens, and his adopted patrician name acts as a ticket of admission into important circles.

Sitting astride the Isthmus of Corinth connecting the Pelopponese peninsula to the Greek mainland, the city of Corinth holds a strategic location. This site was already inhabited by 3000 BC, and Corinth exerted an important role during the glory days of Greek civilization. As capital of the Achaean League, Corinth made the fatal mistake of opposing the growing power of Rome. At the end of the Third Punic War in 146 BC, General Lucius Mummius destroyed the city of Corinth. The Roman practice was to sow salt into the ruins of a defeated city, so that nothing could grow there ever again. However, this site was just too important to let lie, and after a hundred years, in 44 BC, Julius Caesar reestablished Corinth as a Roman colony populated by veterans from his civil war with Pompey the Great.

After disappointing responses from the pagans of Philippi and Athens, and from the Jews of Thessalonica, Paul finds a very receptive audience in Corinth. He spends a long time here, which Luke specifies as a full year and a half (Acts 18:11).

"By trade they were tentmakers" (Acts 18:3). While in Corinth, Paul stays with a couple named Aquila and Priscilla, who were originally from Pontus in Asia Minor, not far from Paul's own home province of Cilicia. They also share a common trade, as tentmakers. Now the common practice among rabbis of the First Century was to learn a trade so that they could support themselves and their families without having to rely on an income from the people they taught. Paul studied in the best rabbinical school in Jerusalem as a youth, but after his conversion, he went back to Tarsus and worked as a tentmaker for ten years, before being called as an evangelist. Similarly, the apostles went back to fishing after the death of Jesus and were summoned back into ministry by the Risen Lord. The fact that rabbis and the apostles were close to the working poor grounded the early Christian and Rabbinic movements in the life of their people and is part of the reason for their historical survival, while other movements of the time disappeared.

One school of rabbinical thought considered tentmaking to be a ritually impure profession, because of the handling of the skins of dead animals. The making of cloth tents, however, brought no stigma with it, and carried some special significance since the Israelites dwelt in tents for forty years of wandering in the desert, and the Lord God himself dwelt in a tent erected according to the instructions of the Torah.

"Claudius had commanded all the Jews to leave Rome" (Acts 18:2). The Roman historian Suetonius confirms as historical fact that, in about 49 AD, the Emperor Claudius "expelled Jews from Rome because of their constant disturbances impelled by Chrestus" *(Impulsore Chresto)*. Seemingly, their discord arose over the new Christian movement, and the Emperor chose to ban them all and let them sort out the matter between themselves elsewhere.

Jews born in Rome were Roman citizens and, when expelled from the city of Rome itself, they would likely settle in a Roman colony with fellow citizens. Jews elsewhere in the empire were honored to receive the Roman exiles into their communities, opening their homes and their synagogues to them. So, Aquila and Priscilla, instead of going back to their native Pontus, initially went instead with many of their friends to the important Roman colony of Corinth. At the time that Paul meets them, Aquila and Priscilla have only been in exile one year, and their exile will last a total of five years, until the death of Claudius in AD 54.

The scattering of the Jews of Rome throughout the world meant that the Roman Christian community occupied not just a single city but a network covering many parts of the entire Empire. The God-fearing non-Jews of Rome, such as Cornelius and his family, kept the home church alive, but the Jewish Christians of Rome acted as a leaven everywhere. Paul and many others encounter them and come away greatly impressed: "your faith is proclaimed in all the world" (Romans 1:8). The communities of the early church were not hermetically sealed from one another but shared a universal vision of the coming kingship of the Lord.

"Silas and Timothy arrived from Macedonia" (Acts 18:5). Paul had arrived in Athens without Timothy, whom he had sent to check up on Jason and the Thessalonians. Apparently, Paul now arrives in Corinth without Timothy or Silas, because they have been sent on yet another mission to Macedonia. On one of these missions, Timothy delivered the First Letter to the Thessalonians and, on another mission, he delivered the Second. Corinth was the venue where Paul begins to write his inspired letters which eventually become part of the New Testament.

During Paul's stay in Corinth, bad news came from the Holy Land. In April of AD 51, Samaritans ambushed some Galilean Jews in transit through their territory at festival time. Eleasar, son of Dineus, led a Jewish mob plundering Samaritan villages. Prefect Cumanus armed the Samaritans and attacked the Jewish force. The Samaritans appeal to Governor Ummidius Quadratus of Syria, then in Tyre, who visited Samaria, Lydda, and Jerusalem. He ordered all parties to Rome for judgment—Prefect, Tribune, Samaritan, and Jewish leaders, including the High Priest. What Jew, whether a follower of Jesus or not, would not grieve over the High Priest being taken in chains to Rome for judgment?

"But when Gallio was proconsul of Achaia" (Acts 18:12). Opponents of Paul take the occasion of the arrival of a new proconsul to bring charges against Paul. Roman civil servants began their term of service on the first day of January, and during his eighteen months in Corinth, Paul saw two Januaries come and go. The legal hassle seems to have taken place at the second January, in the Year AD 52.

Remember that back in Cyprus, Paul and Barnabas had converted the proconsul Sergius Paulus, and the new proconsul Gallio could easily be made aware of the sponsorship that the other proconsul had offered to Paul, who now bore the name of a Roman patrician. Gallio could ask his clerk, "Who is this appearing before me? A Paullus? Is he a member of the aristocracy? What is going on here?" The proconsul refuses to try a Roman citizen on charges brought by non-citizens and proclaims that his court has no jurisdiction over Jewish religious matters. The magistrate knows that these people have been expelled from Rome because of their bickering and he is not about to be drawn into their quarrels.

"Paul was about to open his mouth" (Acts 18:14). Some of the Greek city-states, like Sparta, had been ruled by tyrants, while others, like Corinth and Athens, invented a democratic form of government. Greek democracy was not a perfect institution—women and slaves had no right to vote—but all free men in the city- state had the freedom to attend and address the urban meetings. The art of public speaking *(rhetoric)* fostered a citizenry that knew how to speak in public and was skilled enough to act as their own attorneys in a court of law.

Paul had the rhetorical skills to defend himself before the bench (in Greek, *bema*) of the newly named proconsul Gallio, but it did not come to that. The proconsul would have heard a worthy self-defense from Paul, who as an author displays not just a general, but a conscious and technical knowledge of classical rhetoric. In his writings to Corinth, Paul uses seven rhetorical terms with technical precision:

1) *Apodeixis* — Demonstration (1 Corinthians 2:4)
2) *Syncrisis* — Comparison (1 Corinthians 2:13)
3) *Apologia* — Self-defense (1 Corinthians 9:3)
4) *Typoi* — Types (1 Corinthians 10:6, 11)
5) *Anamenesis* — Recollection (1 Corinthians 11:24–25)
6) *Ainigma* — Enigma (1 Corinthians 13:12)
7) *Hermeneia* — Explanation (1 Corinthians 14:26)

That spring, the Emperor Claudius passes judgment on all the leaders sent to him from the Holy Land. He orders the Samaritan leaders put to death for obstructing the Jewish transit. He banishes the former Prefect Cumanus to exile outside of Italy, a serious penalty for a member of the Roman aristocracy. He sends the tribune Celer back to Jerusalem in disgrace to be beheaded. He also appoints a new Prefect, Antonius Felix (Acts 23). The Jewish High Priest seems to get off lightly on this occasion, so the Jews throughout the world breathe a sigh of relief.

In the summer of that year, Paul, Aquila, and Priscilla leave Corinth for Cenchreae (Acts 18:18) and Ephesus (Acts 18:19), where Aquila and Priscilla remain. Paul continues on to Caesarea (Acts 18:19), and gives a report on his second missionary journey, and then returns to Antioch where he spends nearly two years.

Paul and Sosthenes (1 Corinthians 1:1) — Paul seems to be accompanied later in his travels by the synagogue leader from Corinth, who was beaten by the mob in full view of the court (Acts 18:17). If this is the same Sosthenes, he like Paul would have a vested interest in corresponding with the community back home in Corinth. The Corinthian community remains close to Paul's heart, and at the beginning of his third missionary journey he writes ahead, reminding them of his teachings and how they should behave. Before the surviving letter called First Corinthians, Paul had sent at least one other letter, which has been lost. The Holy Spirit moved the Corinthians to preserve this later letter, and not the prior one, and thus shaped the eventual canon of the New Testament.

"By the name of our Lord Jesus Christ" (1 Corinthians 1:10) — During the first ten verses of First Corinthians, Paul repeats the name of Jesus nine times. This is also a classic rhetorical technique, called "repetition," which is one of the major figures of speech. When a word or phrase recurs at regular intervals, listeners become drawn into the speaker's own thought world. Aristotle said that repetition was a fault of composition, unless used purposely for a particular effect. Paul does precisely that. Saint John Chrysostom comments, "No man whatever, neither apostle nor teacher, but rather the very Desired One is the One he remembered, setting himself as if to rouse those who were heavy-headed after some debauch. For nowhere in any other epistle does the name of Christ occur so frequently. Here it is, many times in a few verses, and by means of it he weaves together, one may say, the whole of the introduction" (Saint John Chrysostom [AD 344–407], in *Patrologia Graecae,* [Paris: J. P. Migne, 1885], Vol. 61, p. 18)

"The word of the cross" (1 Corinthians 1:18) — The conjunction of "word" and "cross" appears three times in the opening pages of First Corinthians:

* "The word of the cross is folly to those who are perishing, but to us who are being saved it is the power of God" (1 Corinthians 1:18),
* "We preach Christ crucified" (1 Corinthians 1:23),
* "I decided to know nothing among you except Jesus Christ and him crucified" (1 Corinthians 2:2).

"For Christ did not send me to baptize but to preach the gospel, and not with eloquent wisdom, lest the cross of Christ be emptied of its power" (1 Corinthians 1:17). In this verse, the word *stauros* "cross" appears for the first time in the epistle, and in the next verse it enters into close embrace with the word *logo* "word." In fact this relationship is so critical that Paul scorns a "word" without the "cross" which without Christ is powerless (1 Corinthians 1:17) but praises the word of the cross in the following verse: "For the word of the cross is folly to those who are perishing, but to us who are being saved it is the power of God" (1 Corinthians 1:18).

The logic of this world finds power in self-glorification and self-gratification, but the logic of the cross is salvation through humility. The Holy Cross is the very logic of Christianity. See how much God loved us; see how the Son of God humbled himself; see the means by which we were saved; see the pattern by which we should model our lives; see the only source of remedy for the world's ills.

"Paul or Apollos or Cephas" (1 Corinthians 3:22) — The Corinthian community seems to know three principal evangelizers at this time, and interestingly, one of them is Peter (Cephas). Once before, in 1 Corinthians 1:12, the same three names appeared in the same sequence. It seems ill mannered for Paul to list himself first and Peter last. Here again is a classical Greek figure of speech called *anabasis*, or "ascent." Paul thinks of himself as lower than Apollos, and Apollos as lower than Peter. Hence, the sequence indicates a kind of ascent, leading up and away from Paul to Peter. Paul's ultimate goal is to point up and away from all three to Christ, lifted high upon the cross. As he says, "This is how one should regard us, as servants of Christ and stewards of the mysteries of God" (1 Corinthians 4:1). Paul then launches into a lengthy review of his moral teachings, which reveal much about the social structure and cultural life of the Corinthians. He asserts this not as his own opinion but under the mantle of divine authority: "And I think that I have the Spirit of God" (1 Corinthians 7:40). At the end of the second reading at Mass, the lector does not say "The word of Paul," but rather, "The Word of the Lord." And, the congregation answers "Thanks be to God."

The Apostles' adventure began as an encounter of people who are open to one another. For the disciples, it was the beginning of a direct acquaintance with the Teacher, seeing where he was staying and starting to get to know him. Indeed, they were not to proclaim an idea, but to witness to a person.

Before being sent out to preach, they had to "be" with Jesus (Mark 3:14), establishing a personal relationship with him. On this basis, evangelization was to be no more than the proclamation of what they felt and an invitation to enter into the mystery of communion with Christ.

Pope Benedict XVI, *General Audience,* (March 22, 2006)

1. What was Paul doing in Corinth, and how did God encourage him?

Acts 18:1–5	
Acts 18:9–10	

2. Describe Apollos and his actions. Acts 18:24–19:1

3. What are believers called to become? And how can this be achieved?

1 Corinthians 1:1–2	
CCC 1695	
CCC 2699	

4. What significance is the "cross of Christ?"

1 Corinthians 1:18	
1 Corinthians 2:2	
CCC 616	
CCC 617	
CCC 618	

5. How could you discuss the mysteries of God?

1 Corinthians 1:25	
CCC 272	
CCC 273	

6. How could you obtain true wisdom?

1 Corinthians 2:1–16	
Wisdom 9:13–18	

7. What should be the foundation of your faith? 1 Corinthians 3:1–13

8. Explain the final purgation.

1 Corinthians 3:15	
CCC 1030	
CCC 1031	

9. Describe something special about you. 1 Corinthians 3:16–17

* Considering the above, are there any changes you might make?

10. Explain the relationship of the Holy Spirit to you and to the church.

1 Corinthians 3:16–17	
CCC 797	

11. What will happen when the Lord comes in glory? 1 Corinthians 4:1–5

12. How do the apostles receive their mandate, and what mystery did they pass on?

1 Corinthians 4:1	
CCC 859	
CCC 1117	

* Which sacrament provides you with the most grace and strength?

13. How did the apostles handle hardships? 1 Corinthians 4:10–13

14. What are disciples expected to do? 1 Corinthians 4:16

15. What is the substance of the kingdom of God? 1 Corinthians 4:20

16. What problem is identified in 1 Corinthians 5:1–13?

17. Why is incest a serious sin? CCC 2388

18. What happens when people tolerate a little bit of evil? 1 Corinthians 5:6–7

19. What is the underlying attitude of Paul's prayer in 1 Corinthians 1:1–4?

20. What is Paul's hope for the Corinthians? 1 Corinthians 1:5–9

* What hope do you have for those you love?

Monthly Social Activity

This month, your small group will meet for coffee, tea, or a simple breakfast, lunch, or dessert in someone's home. Pray for this social event and for the host or hostess. Try, if at all possible, to attend.

After a short prayer and some time for small talk, write down five things for which you are most grateful to God. Try to share about each of these situations in a five-minute time frame.

Examples:

- ◆ *I thank God for my faith and coming to know God better.*

- ◆ *I thank God for living in a free country.*

- ◆ *I thank God for my family.*

- ◆ *I thank God for the home I live in.*

- ◆ *I thank God for the trials I have endured.*

Chapter 13

The Apostolic Liturgy – AD 52
1 Corinthians 9–16

**For as often as you eat this bread and drink the chalice,
you proclaim the Lord's death until he comes.**
1 Corinthians 11:26

Roman Remembrance — October 15, AD 55 is the first anniversary of the death of Claudius. On that date, Agrippina Junior, mother of the Emperor Nero, begins building the Claudium, a temple of the deified Claudius on the Celian Hill in Rome. By erecting this memorial temple, Agrippina wishes to demonstrate that she has not forgotten her husband, the Emperor Claudius, who was also her uncle. Neither Mosaic Law nor Catholic Canon Law permit the marriage of persons with such a close degree of consanguinity, but Roman Civil Law was more permissive.

The Roman people perceive the building of the temple as an act of continuity and of piety. That the Empress Mother wishes to honor her late husband as well as her currently reigning son is a signal that the imperial family is providing consistent policy. The Roman religion upholds the virtue of piety, which means remembering one's parents and ancestors. Claudius himself erected an Altar of Piety in Rome (the frontispiece is in a museum in Ravenna) to honor the members of the Julio-Claudian family who had gone before him. To remember is an act of piety.

Greco-Roman rhetoricians recall to memory already known facts as an oratorical technique of great power, which goes by the formal name *anamnesis*. Isidore of Seville says that sometimes orators pretend to forget something and then pretend to remember: "Anamnesis is the remembrance of a thing which we pretend ourselves to have forgotten." When trying to teach something new, speakers try to find common ground with their audience by reminding them of things already known. This might involve quoting a well-known proverb or making an allusion to a famous work of literature. That reduces the shock value of the novelty presented and helps people grant assent to the speaker with a good will. This technique helps to turn assent into an act of piety.

Hebrew Remembrance — The entire Jewish religion falls under the umbrella of remembering, which in Hebrew is *Zakar*. Adam and Eve forgot God in the garden, but God did not forget them or their descendants, because of the series of covenants God offered to them. The Old Testament contains many striking prayers and psalms begging God to remember, that is to reward, such people as: Noah (Genesis 8:1), Abraham (Genesis 19:29, Exodus 32:13, Deuteronomy 9:27), Rachel (Genesis 30:22), Isaac and Jacob (Exodus 32:13, Deuteronomy 9:27), the congregation (Psalm 74:2), David (Psalms 38:1, 70:1, 132:1), Jerusalem (Jeremiah 2:2), Jeremiah (Jeremiah 15:15), and Ephraim (Jeremiah 31:20).

Of course, God is not likely to forget. God cannot forget. God knows all things and never forgets anything. The danger is not that the intended person will pass out of God's mind. The purpose of the prayer is that God should take action and intervene on behalf of that person. To remember, then, in Hebrew, means not just to keep present in the mind but to take purposeful action.

Similarly, the Old Testament encourages the people of Israel to remember the Lord (Deuteronomy 8:18, Psalm 77:3, Ecclesiastes 12:1, Jeremiah 51:50, Jonah 2:7, and Zechariah 10:9) and rebukes them when they do not remember Him (Judges 8:34, Isaiah 57:11). The Book of Exodus contains two memorial imperatives:
— Remember this day (Passover) when you went forth from Egypt (Exodus 13:3).
— Remember the sabbath day, to keep it holy (Exodus 20:8).

The purpose of Jewish remembrance is not just to keep alive the memory but also to translate the memory into action. The keeping of the feast means the keeping of the commandments. The mutual remembrance of God and Israel is the mutual keeping of the obligations of the covenant. Therefore, the noun "covenant" is often the direct object of the verb "remember"—remember the covenant (Genesis 9:15, Exodus 2:24, Leviticus 26:42, Psalm 105:8, Jeremiah 14:21, and Ezekiel 16:60).

Remembrance has special significance for the Jews, because they have received so many signs and wonders. They simply have more wonderful things to remember. At Passover time particularly the Israelites have a sacred duty to keep remembrance of the favors granted to them in being brought safely out of captivity in Egypt. They saw God's glory, His miracles in Egypt, the pillar of cloud by day, the pillar of fire by night, the smoke on the mountaintop, the glowing face of Moses.

Christian Remembrance — The Good Thief asks Jesus to remember him when He enters into His kingdom (Luke 23:42). In so doing, he acknowledges his belief that Jesus is the long-awaited Hebrew Messiah, and more. Christian remembrance grows out of the matrix of Jewish memorial.

Jesus and the apostles remembered the saving deeds of God from the Hebrew Bible and celebrated the festival days. By remembering the former covenant, they brought into being a new one. Whereas the Passover meal memorialized the crossing of the Red Sea by Moses and his nation, the Christian liturgy memorializes the passage from death to life of Jesus and all those bonded to Him.

Christianity grows seamlessly out of Judaism by means of remembrance. Never at any moment in the life of Christ or of the apostles did they forget the great heritage in whose shadow they emerged. Christ never forgot Moses; the apostles never forgot Moses or Jesus. The Mosaic memorial meal morphed miraculously into the Christian Eucharist.

The pages of the New Testament contain five different accounts of the Last Supper, from Matthew, Mark, Luke, John, and Paul's First Letter to the Corinthians. These five authors remembered as they wrote and recorded to help others remember. Luke and Paul bring out the aspects of remembrance most explicitly.

And he took bread, and when he had given thanks he broke it and gave it to them, saying, "This is my body which is given for you. Do this in remembrance of me." And likewise the chalice after supper, saying, "This chalice which is poured out for you is the new covenant in my blood." Luke 22:19–20	For I received from the Lord what I also delivered to you, that the Lord Jesus on the night when he was betrayed took bread, and when he had given thanks, he broke it, and said, "This is my body which is for you. Do this in remembrance of me." In the same way also the chalice, after supper, saying, "This chalice is the new covenant in my blood. Do this as often as you drink it, in remembrance of me." 1 Corinthians 11:23–25

First Corinthians has two memorial imperatives, one after each consecration. Luke retains only the first of these, standing in the middle between the two consecrations. The Roman Liturgy has only a single memorial imperative also, standing at the end and pointing back to both consecrations.

Clearly, these two accounts belong to the same liturgical tradition, just as the accounts of Matthew and Mark belong to another tradition. The greatest antiquity belongs to the account in First Corinthians, one of the earliest apostolic documents, datable to Paul's second missionary journey around AD 53 and contemporary with an early phase of gospel formation. This letter contains several quotes of Jesus called "Jesus' sayings." The most fully developed of these materials is the Last Supper narrative, which can be characterized with equanimity as the only gospel pericope preserved intact in an earlier context, embedded within one of the early epistles. No pericope within any of the four gospels can be dated with the same degree of certainty as this one, which survives in a pre-editorial condition not far removed from its free-floating state.

Paul wrote to the Corinthians only twenty-four years after the Last Supper had actually taken place and a couple of decades before Matthew, Luke, or John were written down. Therefore, Paul's is the best testimony to the shape of the primitive liturgy, which by his account attached explicit memorial to the consecration of both the bread and the cup.

Did Jesus say, "Do this in memory of Me?" once (as recorded in Luke) or twice (as in Paul)? One school of exegesis wants to reduce all doublings, giving the benefit of the doubt to the shorter expression. This literary practice should respect the uses of repetition to good purpose everywhere.

"As often as you eat this bread and drink this cup" (1 Corinthians 11:26) — Paul's Last Supper narrative ends with a transitional verse that has found its way into the liturgies of the church. Paul's text proclaims the death and return of the Lord. In the ancient

Syrian liturgy, the Lord speaks about His own death and return. In the modern Roman liturgy, the people acclaim the Lord's memory.

1 Corinthians 11:26	Syrian Liturgy	Roman Liturgy
For as often as you eat this bread and drink the chalice, you proclaim the Lord's death until he comes.	When you eat this bread and drink this cup you proclaim My death until I come.	When we eat this bread and drink this cup we proclaim your death, O Lord, until you come again.

Clearly, this verse, in each of its manifestations, teaches the unity between the sacrament and the sacrifice. The meal is a memorial of the death of Christ and will continue to be so from the time of His death until the time of His return in glory.

To consume the meal heedlessly would be a sacrilege. "For any one who eats and drinks without discerning the body eats and drinks judgment upon himself" (1 Corinthians 11:28). Apparently, some of the Corinthians had fallen into selfish or unreflective participation in the Eucharistic service. Paul finds this offensive, no doubt because of the great Passover tradition in which he was reared, whereby the poor and those without families were given hospitality during the Seder meal. He uses strong language, because he is conscious of liturgical abuses. Strict adherence to the spirit of the liturgy was especially important in apostolic times, because they were setting the standards for all generations to come.

"So faith, hope, love abide, these three" (1 Corinthians 13:13). Disbelief, despair, and hatred have no place in the Eucharistic banquet, and so Paul follows his discussion of the apostolic liturgy with a beautiful hymn in honor of divine love and proceeds to enumerate the three theological virtues, pure divine gifts from on high. He encourages us to "earnestly desire the higher gifts" (1 Corinthians 12:31). Faith, hope, and love do exist in a natural form, as actual graces, but in their supernatural form they are God's own life communicated to us by the power of the Spirit. Why would anyone be satisfied with natural hope, when God offers the gift of supernatural hope as well? Even among the supernatural gifts, one of them is greatest. Faith and hope only act as guides on the path towards heaven, but love is already a participation in unending heavenly life. Faith and hope lead us to enter into the liturgy, but the liturgy, properly speaking, is a celebration of divine love.

"When you come, each one has a hymn, a lesson, a revelation, a tongue, or an interpretation" (1 Corinthians 14:26). Paul describes a very early state of liturgical development, when the Holy Spirit was using the congregation to establish the shape of the celebration. Another early document which describes this process is the *Didache*, (Teaching of the Twelve Apostles), which lays forth the rubrics of the apostolic liturgy and then makes allowance for those who are inspired. The history of the liturgy affords long periods of tradition punctuated by inspired periods of development. Among the saints who contributed to the development of the liturgy were Gregory in Rome, Ambrose in Milan, John Chrysostom in Constantinople, Ephraim in Syria, and Cyril and Methodius in the Slavic lands. These fathers and patriarchs possessed the intuition of how God wanted to be worshipped and made it possible for whole nations to participate worthily in divine service, their reverent liturgy.

"If Christ has not been raised, then our preaching is in vain and your faith is in vain" (1 Corinthians 15:14). In the end, the entire Christian life depends upon the Risen Lord. Paul says, "he appeared to more than five hundred brethren at one time, most of whom are still alive" (1 Corinthians 15:6). Because Christ is risen, death is defeated. Humanity itself is changed, putting off mortality, and becoming clothed in immortality. The Resurrection of the Lord is the great mystery over everything, enabling the liturgy to be the reception of the Body and Blood of the One who once died but is now alive. Paul celebrated this liturgy and this mystery with the Corinthian community, with their first converts in the household of Stephanas, with the transitory refugees Aquila and Prisca, with the great preacher Apollos, and with his secretary and faithful companions Timothy and Sosthenes. In a touchingly beautiful valedictory, Paul wishes them all the grace of the Lord Jesus and his own love in Christ Jesus (1 Corinthians 16:23–24).

The Church draws her life from the Eucharist. This truth does not simply express a daily experience of faith, but recapitulates *the heart of the mystery of the Church*. In a variety of ways she joyfully experiences the constant fulfillment of the promise: "Lo, I am with you always, to the close of the age" (Matthew 28:20), but in the Holy Eucharist, through the changing of bread and wine into the body and blood of the Lord, she rejoices in this presence with unique intensity. Ever since Pentecost, when the Church, the People of the New Covenant, began her pilgrim journey towards her heavenly homeland, the Divine Sacrament has continue to mark the passing of her days, filling them with confident hope.

The Second Vatican Council rightly proclaimed that the Eucharistic sacrifice is "the source and summit of the Christian life. For the most holy Eucharist contains the Church's entire spiritual wealth: Christ himself, our Passover and living bread. Through his own flesh, now made living and life-giving by the Holy Spirit, he offers life to men." Consequently the gaze of the Church is constantly turned to her Lord, present in the Sacrament of the Altar, in which she discovers the full manifestation of his boundless love. … In the humble signs of bread and wine, changed into his body and blood, Christ walks beside us as our strength and our food for the journey, and he enables us to become, for everyone, witnesses of hope.

John Paul II, *Ecclesia de Eucharistia* (April 17, 2003), 1, 62

1. How should a servant of God be supported? 1 Corinthians 9:1–18, CCC 2122

2. What is the nature of a minister of God? 1 Corinthians 9:19–27, CCC 876

3. What does Paul demonstrate in 1 Corinthians 10:1–11? CCC 129

4. How can you overcome severe temptation? 1 Corinthians 10:12–13, CCC 2848

5. List names for the activity in 1 Corinthians 10:16–17. CCC 1329–1331

6. What does the Eucharist do? 1 Corinthians 10:16–18, CCC 1396

7. What motivates Christians? 1 Corinthians 10:31–11:1

8. How should you approach liturgy? 1 Corinthians 11:17–22, CCC 2178

9. Compare the following passages from Sacred Scripture.

Matthew 26:26–28	
Mark 14:22–24	
Luke 22:17–19	
1 Corinthians 11:23–26	

10. What must you do before Communion? 1 Corinthians 11:27–34, CCC 1385

11. Find nine spiritual gifts in 1 Corinthians 12:1–11. Circle the ones you have.

12. How can you discern these charisms, and for what purpose? CCC 799–801

13. List the spiritual gifts found in 1 Corinthians 12:27–31. Which do you have?

14. Describe the attributes of a loving person. Circle those that describe you.

Love is _____ *and* _____ ;

love is not _____ *or* _____ ;

it is not _____ *or* _____ .

Love does not insist on _____ _____ _____ ;

it is not _____ *or* _____ ;

it does not rejoice at _____ , *but rejoices in the* _____ .

Love _____ *all things,* _____ *all things,* _____

all things, _____ *all things.* *1 Corinthians 13:4–7*

15. Explain the purpose of tongues and prophecy. 1 Corinthians 14:1–25

* Have you ever experienced the gifts of prophecy or tongues in worship? Please share with your small group.

16. Where does the church draw its life? 1 Corinthians 14:26–33, CCC 752

17. Describe the most significant event of human history.

Psalm 16:9–11	
Acts 2:30–31	
1 Corinthians 15:3–5	
CCC 639	
CCC 651–652	

18. What is the final enemy of man?

1 Corinthians 15:20–28	
CCC 1008	

19. How is Christ's Resurrection different from Lazarus' rising from the dead?

1 Corinthians 15:35–50	
CCC 646	

20. What will happen to you after death?

1 Corinthians 15:51–58	
CCC 997	
CCC 998	
CCC 999	

* Write a paraphrase of the proverb in 1 Corinthians 15:33 in your own words.

The heavenly sacrifice, instituted by Christ, is the most gracious legacy of his new covenant. On the night he was delivered up to be crucified he left us this gift as a pledge of his abiding presence.

This sacrifice is our sustenance on life's journey; by it we are nourished and supported along the road of life until we depart from this world and make our way to the Lord... It was the Lord's will that his gifts should remain with us, and that we who have been redeemed by his precious blood should constantly be sanctified according to the pattern of his own passion. And so he commanded those faithful disciples of his whom he made the first priests of his Church to enact these mysteries of eternal life continuously. All priests throughout the churches of the world must celebrate these mysteries until Christ comes again from heaven...

It is appropriate that we should receive the body of Christ in the form of bread, because, as there are many grains of wheat in the flour from which bread is made by mixing it with water and baking it with fire, so also we know that many members make up the one body of Christ which is brought to maturity by the fire of the Holy Spirit.

Saint Gaudentius of Brescia, (–410AD) *Sermon*, Tract 2, 68.30.

Chapter 14

Ephesians — AD 54–57
Acts 19, Ephesians

**Blessed be the God and Father of our Lord Jesus Christ,
who has blessed us in Christ with every spiritual blessing in the heavenly
places, even as he chose us in him before the foundation of the world,
that we should be holy and blameless before him.
He destined us in love to be his sons through Jesus Christ,
according to the purpose of his will,
to the praise of his glorious grace which he freely bestowed on us in the Beloved.**
Ephesians 1:3–6

It was inevitable that Paul in the course of his wide travels would encounter the important pilgrimage center of Ephesos (usually spelled with the borrowed Latin ending *–us*, instead of the proper Greek ending *–os*). This Ionian city was located at the strategic mouth of the Kayster Valley, one of four major river routes into the rich interior of Asia Minor, each with a great port city at its mouth:

RIVER	PORT CITY
Kayster (Lesser Meander) River	Ephesos
(Greater) Meander River	Miletos
Hermos River	Smyrna
Kaykus River	Pergamon

For these four ports, the conjunction of sea and river trade created bustling commercial activity as described by the geographer Strabo in 23 BC. Cyrus the Great, who established the Persian Empire, absorbed the territory of Asia Minor in 546 BC. The Persians made Sardis (*Sepharad*) in Asia Minor the seat of a satrapy and the western terminus of the royal road, from their Persian capital city of Susa. Jewish merchants followed that road and established a presence in the area, attested within the pages of the Bible as early as the Fifth Century BC (Obadiah 20). The Jewish community there was so large that it eventually gave its name to all of Mediterranean Jewry, called "Sephardic."

Emperor Augustus favored Ephesos over her competitors and designated her the capital city of the Roman province of Asia after 30 BC. Both Jews and God-fearers from Ephesos were in Jerusalem sixty years later for the first Pentecost to receive the Holy Spirit (Acts 2:9). Paul is magnetically attracted to this important community but he circles around it, not coming directly from the east, but skirting around on the north and approaching it from the west. Only after a year and a half in Corinth does Paul finally go to Ephesos, but eventually he spends three years there (Acts 20:31), longer there than any of his other mission churches.

"Into what were you baptized?" (Acts 19:3). Upon his arrival, Paul discovers twelve disciples of John the Baptist, whom he re-baptizes "in the name of the Lord Jesus" (Acts 19:5), even though elsewhere he says that his ministry was not to baptize but to preach. The Sacrament of Baptism can be conferred only once, but the baptism of John was not the Sacrament instituted by Christ. John's baptism was an outward expression of repentance for sin, but not yet the reception of forgiveness. Note how far spread the disciples of the Baptizer are, all the way to Ephesos. John the Baptist's movement could have become a great world religion if he had promoted himself and not been beheaded. In fact, he deferred to Jesus and wished only to be the precursor of the founder. This group could be called a synagogue of followers of John the Baptist (ten adult males was the minimum requirement for a synagogue). Paul makes it a Catholic church.

"God did extraordinary miracles by the hands of Paul" (Acts 19:11). The Greeks had a cult of healing, with shrines to the healing god Asklepios scattered throughout the Greek world. The big shrine was at Pergamon, to the north. Eventually the science of medicine would arise from the anecdotal information collected about the care and treatment of sufferers at the Asklepion in Pergamon. However, medicine was not yet a science but still a branch of pagan worship. Paul's miracles of healing constituted no threat to anyone, because everyone was still struggling to find a way to cope with illness. To the credit of the Ephesians, they were just as interested in the exorcisms as in the physical healings. Ephesos was an ancient center of magic lore and of such influence that books of magic were called the genre of "Ephesian writing." With the triumph of the works of God through the hands of Paul, the Ephesians, who practiced black arts, gathered and burned their extremely valuable magic tomes. Ephesos remained an important center of book learning, however. Sixty years later, the Roman patrician Titus Iulius Aquila built one of the great libraries of the ancient world there, the Library of Celsus, in memory of his father, the Roman governor Titus Iulius Candidus Marius (Celsus Polemaenus). The New Testament contains several pieces of writing that could be called the "Ephesian Literature" because they are associated with the city—Paul's Letter to the Ephesians, John's Gospel and three letters, and Revelation.

"Great is Artemis of the Ephesians!" (Acts 19:28). The Ephesians boasted a great pilgrimage site, the temple of the goddess of hunting Artemis (called in Latin by the name Diana). In point of fact, the pagan Greeks and Romans did not practice much pilgrimage. Each city had its own local shrine where the people of the place worshipped their own patron god or goddess. So Athena was the patron goddess of Athens, Artemis the patroness of Ephesos, and so forth. The only appreciable sites of international pilgrimage in the Roman Empire were the prophetic oracle of Delphi, the healing shrine of Asklepion of Pergamon, the Artemsion of Ephesos, and the Temple of Jerusalem. Of these, the most visited was Jerusalem and the second was Ephesos, which attracted worshippers from as far away as Britain.

The Artemesion in Paul's time was a massive building of one hundred seventeen columns, each over eighteen meters tall. The sale of idols to pilgrims was a major source of income for the people of Ephesos. Wealthy pilgrims could purchase large statues and have them shipped home, while the poorer devotees could scrimp and save to buy an amulet to put around their necks. Such tiny images of the goddess have been found as far away as Germany and Britain. Jews were horrified at the proliferation of graven images but kept their distance in silence. Paul, on the other hand, tried to convert the pagan Ephesians, teaching them in their own words, "Gods made with hands are not gods" (Acts 19:26). We do note create gods; God created us. As Paul later writes to the Ephesians, "For we are his workmanship, created in Christ Jesus for good works, which God prepared beforehand, that we should walk in them" (Ephesians 2:10).

"They rushed together into the theater" (Acts 19:29). The rioters use their theater as a meeting place. Pilgrims to Ephesos today are shown the massive theater, three levels of twenty-two tiers, capable of holding nearly 25,000 spectators. In Paul's time the theater stood on that location, but what is visible now was completed under Trajan, fifty years after Paul's visit there. What a suitable place for idolaters to riot! Idolatry is a fraud. Hypocrites sell false gods. The word "hypocrite" in Greek means "one who puts himself before the critics," that is to say, "a play actor." So those who only feared the loss of their income from the gullible pilgrims use the stage to forment violence against Paul and his companions.

"He is our peace, who has made us both one" (Ephesians 2:14). The relationship between Ephesos and Jerusalem was one of competition but little real antagonism. Two great religious systems, classical paganism and Judaism, each had name recognition and product loyalty from their own clientele. Jews went to Ephesos for trade but not for religion. A few pagans went to Jerusalem for trade, but a larger number, the God-fearers, went for religious purposes. Paul's preaching provokes a near riot that ends peaceably and then the process of reconciliation begins between Greeks and Jews in Christ: "And he came and preached peace to you who were far off and peace to those who were near; for through him we both have access in one Spirit to the Father. So then you are no longer strangers and sojourners, but you are fellow citizens with the saints and members of the household of God, built upon the foundation of the apostles and the prophets, Christ Jesus himself being the cornerstone" (Ephesians 2:17–20). The cornerstone of many a Catholic church contains the great verse, "One Lord, one faith, one baptism, one God and Father of us all," (Ephesians 4:5–6) from this letter. Paul uses architectural imagery to describe the church, in part because Ephesos was home to one of the great buildings of antiquity.

"When he ascended on high he led a host of captives" (Ephesians 4:8). Paul does not quote the Old Testament frequently in his letter to the Ephesians, because many of them are Gentile converts without biblical literacy. He finally cannot resist quoting Psalm 68:18, however, because the Ascension of Our Lord is one of the great teachings of his letter. The Temple of Artemis was located in a swamp, a low spot originally by the sea shore before the silting up of the delta left Ephesos stranded three miles inland. Paul teaches that Christ descended into the depths to release those captive there and led them heavenwards. Therefore, "speaking the truth in love, we are to grow up in every way into him who is the head, into Christ" (Ephesians 4:15). The remains of the church of Saint John the Evangelist in Ephesos in fact appears on a hilltop, overlooking the ruins of the Artemis temple, Christianity looking down upon paganism. In point of fact, the Christian movement led the people of Ephesos to worship on a higher level, into the fullness of truth. The triumph of Christianity there, where false religion was good business, was a miracle of the Spirit—"and raised us up with him into the heavenly places in Christ Jesus" (Ephesians 2:6).

"I bow my knees before the Father" (Ephesians 3:14). The first half of the Letter to the Ephesians is filled with familiar references from the other Pauline letters, making it a kind of concordance or synopsis of his teaching. The teaching on salvation through grace is here: "by grace you have been saved" and "by grace you have been saved through faith" (Ephesians 2:5, 8), and also in Galatians and Romans. The devout intercession on behalf of the readers (Ephesians 3:14) resembles the hymn of self-emptying from Philippians. There are so many cross references that some scholars conclude that the letter is forgery, but the familiar material keeps getting recombined in clever ways and soaring to heights of authentic mysticism: "to know the love of Christ which surpasses knowledge, that you may be filled with the fullness of God" (Ephesians 3:19). To this community where Paul spent the most time teaching, he can present an advanced lesson in Christianity, making only passing references to the basic teachings while pointing onwards to "the breadth and length and height and depth" (Ephesians 3:18), which he summarizes simply in the single word "mystery," which appears more often in Ephesians than in any other book of the Bible. The mystery is what God revealed (Ephesians 1:9, 3:3), and what we have come to know (Ephesians 3:4). It gives us fellowship (Ephesians 3:9), for it is nothing less than the mystery of the gospel (Ephesians 6:19), as exemplified by Christian matrimony, "This mystery is a profound one, and I am saying that it refers to Christ and the church" (Ephesians 5:32).

"Be subject to one another out of reverence for Christ" (Ephesians 5:21). The many practical exhortations to wives and husbands, children and parents, servants and masters, derive from this one principle—to practice obedience in every aspect of our lives out of love for Christ. Modern readers accuse Paul of endorsing sexism, authoritarianism, and even slavery in the last two chapters of Ephesians. These critics have failed to meditate on the chapter heading: "Be subject to one another" (Ephesians 5:21). Mutual care and respect are essential to the harmony of human relationships, regardless of what social institutions may exist at the time. Paul did not invent, excuse, or prolong slavery. Paul did not condone, rationalize, or excuse spousal or child abuse. Rather, he tried to fortify people with the encouragement of God, to take courage and bring the spirit of Christ into every human relationship. In this way, Paul helped to bring about the transformation of society, planting seeds that bore fruit, some right away, and some many centuries later. Paul was part of the solution, not part of the problem, because he identified the true enemy: "For we are not contenders against flesh and blood, but against the principalities, against the powers, against the world rulers of this present darkness, against the spiritual hosts of wickedness in the heavenly places" (Ephesians 6:12). Paul sends his beloved Ephesians into this spiritual battle vested with the belt of truth, the breastplate of righteousness, the shield of faith, the sandals of peace, the helmet of salvation, and the sword of the Spirit. He himself, an ambassador in chains, asks for nothing but prayers that he may open his mouth boldly to proclaim the mystery of the gospel. What an apostle!

In the love-story recounted by the bible, he [the Lord] comes towards us, he seeks to win our hearts, all the way to the Last Supper, to the piercing of his heart on the Cross, to his appearances after the Resurrection and to the great deeds by which, through the activity of the Apostles, he guided the nascent Church along its path. Nor has the Lord been absent from subsequent Church history; he encounters us ever anew, in the men and women who reflect his presence, in his word, in the sacraments, and especially in the Eucharist. In the Church's Liturgy, in her prayer, in the living community of believers, we experience the love of God, we perceive his presence and we thus learn to recognize that presence in our daily lives.

He has loved us first and he continues to do so; we too, then, can respond with love. God does not command of us a feeling, which we ourselves are incapable of producing. He loves us, he makes us see and experience his love, and since he has "loved us first," love can also blossom as a response within us.

In the gradual unfolding of this encounter, it is clearly revealed that love is not merely a sentiment. Sentiments come and go. A sentiment can be a marvelous first spark, but it is not the fullness of love. … mature love calls into play all man's potentialities. … The love-story between God and man consists in the very fact that this communion of will increases in a communion of thought and sentiment, and thus our will and God's will increasingly coincide: God's will is no longer for me an alien will … but it is now my own will, based on the realization that God is in fact more deeply present to me than I am to myself. Then self-abandonment to God increases and God becomes our joy. … Love grows through love.

Pope Benedict XVI, *Deus Caritas Est* (December 25, 2005) 17–18

1. Describe some facts about Paul's third missionary journey.

Acts 18:18–22	
Acts 19:1	
Acts 20:16–21	
Acts 20:29–32	

* Read the Letter to the Ephesians in one sitting and choose your favorite verse.

2. Complete the table below.

Why did God make us?	Ephesians 1:5–6
What is the glory of God?	CCC 294
What is the purpose of Christ's life?	Ephesians 1:7 CCC 517
What can you hope for?	CCC 2839
What does faith seek?	Ephesians 1:18
What opens the eyes of hearts?	CCC 158
What is Jesus' place and position?	Ephesians 1:18–23 CCC 668

3. Explain the Paschal Mystery.

Ephesians 2:4–7	
CCC 654	

4. How were you saved?

Ephesians 1:7	
Ephesians 2:5	
Ephesians 2:8	
Romans 3:24	

5. Define "Grace."

Ephesians 2:8	
CCC 1996	
CCC 1997	

6. Identify three enemies of the redeemed person from Ephesians 2:1–3.

7. What were you, and what are you now? Ephesians 2:19

8. How was Paul made a minister of the gospel? Ephesians 3:7

9. Fill in the blanks of Paul's prayer from Ephesians 3:14–21.

For this reason I bow my knees before the Father, from whom every family in heaven and on earth is named, that according to the riches of his glory he may grant you to be _____ with _____ through his Spirit in the inner man, and that _____ may _____ in your _____ through _____; that you, being _____ and _____ in _____, may have _____ to _____ with all the saints what is the breadth and ___ _____ and height and _____, and to know the _____ of Christ which surpasses _____, that you may be _____ with ____ _____ the _____ of God.

Now to him who by the _____ at work within us is able to do _____ _____ _____ than all that we _____ or _____, to him be glory in the church and in Christ Jesus to all generations, for ever and ever. Amen.

* Circle one phrase from the above prayer that you most cherish and desire.

10. Explain the unity of the faith.

Ephesians 4:4–6	
CCC 172–173	
CCC 174	
CCC 2790	

11. What can a mature Christian witness do?

Ephesians 4:11–14	
CCC 2044	
CCC 2045	

12. In what practical way could you "Speak the truth in love?" Ephesians 4:15

13. How can you be renewed?

Ephesians 4:20–24	
CCC 1695	

14. What advice can you find in Ephesians 4:25–27?

15. Give the advice found in the following passages.

Ephesians 4:31–32	
Ephesians 5:1–2	
Ephesians 5:6–20	

16. How should a Christian family behave?

Wives		Ephesians 5:21–24
Husbands		Ephesians 5:25–33
Children		Ephesians 6:1–3
Fathers		Ephesians 6:4

* Is there anything above that you could strive to improve?

17. Who and what must Christians contend against? Ephesians 6:10–12

18. Describe the armor of God. Ephesians 6:13–17

19. What command is given in Ephesians 6:18?

20. What does Paul ask of the Ephesians? Ephesians 6:18b–20

Chapter 15

Return to Corinth — AD 57
2 Corinthians

**But we have this treasure in earthen vessels,
to show that the transcendent power belongs to God
and not to us.**
2 Corinthians 4:7

Paul's third missionary journey begins by retracing the second journey in reverse order. Paul visited Ephesos at the end of the second journey, and it becomes one of his first stops on the third journey. The first visit had been frustratingly short. He left Aquila and Priscilla there (Acts 18:19). But, the second stay there is the longest anywhere, three months (Acts 19:8), plus two years (Acts 19:10), which adds up to nearly three years (Acts 20:31). While there, Paul thinks about his other beloved community in Corinth and he begins a series of letters to them:

A first letter now lost (1 Corinthians 5:9) written from Ephesos,
"The First Letter to the Corinthians" written from Ephesos,
another lost letter (2 Corinthians 2:3) written from Ephesos,
"The Second Letter to the Corinthians" written from Philippi.

"I wanted to come to you first" (2 Corinthians 1:15). Paul planned to make Corinth his next stop. "I wanted to visit you on my way to Macedonia, and to come back to you from Macedonia and have you send me on my way to Judea" (2 Corinthians 1:16). He wanted to join the Spring delegations going from those communities to convey the temple tax and donations to Jerusalem. That plan did not work out, however, because Titus failed to return from a mission: "My mind could not rest because I did not find my brother Titus" (2 Corinthians 2:13).

Paul's concern for Titus trumps his plan to visit Corinth and reveals that, while Paul was often demanding with his friends, he was also fiercely loyal. Several letters reveal how useful the Greek convert Titus was to Paul:

accompanying Paul from Antioch to Jerusalem (Galatians 2:1, 3),
being sent to Corinth (2 Corinthians 12:18),
to Macedonia (2 Corinthians 7:5–6),
and to Dalmatia (2 Timothy 4:10),
and being left in Crete (Titus 1:5).

Later, Paul addresses Titus in a short letter, in which Paul calls Titus "my true child in common faith" (Titus 1:4). Oddly, Luke never mentions Titus in the Acts of the Apostles, possibly because of the unfortunate coincidence that in the middle of the year AD 69, a general by the same name, Titus, took command of the Roman forces in Judea, besieging Jerusalem and destroying the temple. This constitutes a hint that the Acts of the Apostles may have been written after that time.

"Was I vacillating ...?" (2 Corinthians 1:17). Paul maintains a flexible schedule while traveling. Though he has his own plan A, he remains open at all times to the Lord's plan B. Back on the second journey, he was kept from preaching in Asia "having been forbidden by the Holy Spirit" (Acts 16:6). He tried to go to Bithynia, "but the Spirit of Jesus did not allow them" (Acts 16:7). Only because of a vision in the night did Paul cross into Europe, "concluding that God had called us to preach the gospel to them" (Acts 16:10). Paul would have been willing to stay longer in Philippi, Thessalonika, and Beroea, but was driven out by riots. As a result, he can spend more time in Corinth and Ephesos. Now again, Paul has to change plans for the sake of Titus. He realizes that this makes him seem unreliable. Paul is embarrassed about failing to follow his planned itinerary, and Second Corinthians seems very much like a letter of apology to people who expected to see him sooner.

"Our word to you has not been Yes and No" (2 Corinthians 1:18). With this sentence, Paul begins one of his most impressive displays of reasoning. He may have changed his plans but never his message. He uses a saying of Jesus found at two other places in the New Testament, which bans the swearing of oaths:

* "Do not swear at all, either by heaven, for it is the throne of God, or by the earth, for it is his footstool, or by Jerusalem, for it is the city of the great King. And do not swear by your head, for you cannot make one hair white or black. Let whatever you say be simply 'Yes' or 'No;' anything more than this comes from evil (Sermon on the Mount, Matthew 5:34–37).
* "But above all, my brethren, do not swear, either by heaven or by earth or with any other oath, but let your yes be yes and your no be no, that you may not fall under condemnation" (James 5:12).

Paul takes this simple moral counsel and turns it into a great Christological teaching. He has always preached Christ, who is the "Yes" to God the Father. Paul invited others to join with him in giving assent to Christ, the Great Amen. First Corinthians already contained several free-floating Jesus sayings:

* on divorce (1 Corinthians 7:10–11; Matthew 5:32; Luke 16:18),
* on support (1 Corinthians 9:14; Matthew 10:10; Luke 10:7),
* on the institution of the Eucharist (1 Corinthians 11:23–26; Matthew 26:26–29; Mark 14:22–25; Luke 22:15–20).

The four gospels have not yet been put to paper, but Paul's two letters to the Corinthians form a seedbed for the germination of gospel materials, showing one way that they circulated in the sphere of the oral gospel.

"We are the aroma of Christ" (2 Corinthians 2:15). Places of worship have particular kinds of smells. Ancient temples, including those in Corinth and Jerusalem, were filled with a heavy, sweet odor, because of the burning of sacrificed animals, plants, and incense. Because they use different kinds of incense, Byzantine churches do not smell the same as Latin churches. People who spend time in such buildings emerge having those particular aromas about them, in the folds of their garments and the pores of their skin. Because Paul had eye problems, his other senses probably became more acute, and he had a keener sense of smell than most. Perhaps, like some of the later saints, he could sense the presence of good or evil by means of smell. In any event, he produces a powerful metaphor when he says, "through us spreads the fragrance of the knowledge of him everywhere" (2 Corinthians 2:14). Christ is the sacrificial offering, and we hover about him like wafts of smoke from burning incense. Others will be drawn to him if we let ourselves be steeped in the odor of sanctity.

"You yourselves are our letter of recommendation" (2 Corinthians 3:2). In a second powerful metaphor, the letter-writer Paul compares his Corinthian correspondents to a letter. Who wrote the letter? Christ. How was it written? In the Spirit. Who delivered the letter? Paul. Who receives the letter? _____ Paul leaves open the answer to that question. In one way, we are a letter from Christ to the world, a letter of invitation to the people of the world to become incorporated into Christ. In another way, we are a letter from Christ to the Father, a letter of introduction to instruct the Father to receive us into his heavenly kingdom.

When ancient people wrote a letter, they would seal it in wax and stamp the wax with the impression from their signet ring. Only the recipient of the letter had the right to break the seal and, as long as the seal was unbroken, no unauthorized person had ever read the letter. So Paul's metaphor that the Corinthians ARE a letter provides the backdrop for the earlier statement, "he has put his seal upon us" (2 Corinthians 1:22). We have been stamped "Property of God," and on the Last Day when the seals are opened and everything that has been hidden is revealed, the message we bear from Christ to the Father will be read aloud to all.

"We bear this treasure in earthen vessels" (2 Corinthians 4:7). In a third metaphor, Paul writes that the grace that fills hearts is a treasure of infinite value, a guarantee of eternal life, but our outer form is still the frail, human condition that is common to us all. When the monks of Qumran, on the shore of the Dead Sea, saw the Roman legions coming to destroy their monastery, they wrapped their precious biblical scrolls and their community documents in skins, inserted them into large earthen water jars, and hid them in caves in the hillsides. Nineteen centuries later, these written treasures were discovered, many of them in an excellent state of preservation because of the protection provided by the earthen jugs. Now the outer vessels were just ordinary pieces of pottery, having no great value, but they protected scrolls of immense spiritual and historic worth. So, our mortal bodies and our flawed selves have become storage containers for the gift of the Holy Spirit. One day we will be transformed into glorious beings for all to see: "but we shall all be changed" (1 Corinthians 15:51). We have already been changed inside, but not yet outwardly, and nonetheless we have the dignity of carrying Christ to the world.

"If the earthly tent we live in is destroyed, we have a building from God" (2 Corinthians 5:1). Paul continues to use metaphors, expressing through various comparisons the great truth of the plan of salvation. Now, he uses a familiar image, for he himself was a tentmaker, along with his friend Aquila, and they had worked together at the making of tents during their shared sojourn in Corinth (Acts 18:3). Many people in the Near East live in tents, both in Paul's time and in the present day. In addition to the Berbers of North Africa and the Bedouin of Arabia, millions of Turks and Iranians still lead migratory lives and remain as tent-dwellers. Just as people live in tents, so our souls dwell in our bodies, and so Paul compares our bodies to tents. Some peoples used tents part of the time, for pasturing their flocks, while returning to regular permanent buildings the rest of the time. So, Paul says, we live in tents now, but we look forward to going to the mansion that has been prepared for us by Jesus in heaven: "In my Father's house are many rooms" (John 14:2).

"Behold, now is the acceptable time" (2 Corinthians 6:2). Commenting on a verse from Isaiah 49:8, Paul highlights that the time in which the Corinthians are living is the privileged moment, the intersection of hope and satisfaction, the meeting between prophecy and fulfillment. That was true of the First Century in general, of course, but what is there about the year AD 57 that makes it special? The Holy Spirit knows and reveals to Paul that this is the lull before the storm. The popular young emperor Nero, only 24 years old, is about to show his true colors and bring about the self-destruction of the Julio-Claudian Dynasty that had ruled the world for a hundred years. No one but the Spirit knows that Rome will burn, that Nero will kill his mother, his teacher, his wife, his child, and the head of the praetorian guard. More obvious to the casual observer is the fragility of peace in the Holy Land, constantly on the verge of civil war between Jews and Samaritans, and of uprising against the Roman occupying force, but who could prophecy that Jerusalem herself would be destroyed only thirteen years hence? Year 57 was the only time when certain things could be done to prepare for the coming disasters. Paul is laying the groundwork for the survival of the Christian religion out of the general catastrophe to strike both Rome and the Holy Land.

"God loves a cheerful giver" (2 Corinthians 9:7). Paul wants the churches of Macedonia and Achaia to exceed themselves in generosity, donating not only the temple tax that all Jews had to send to the temple in Jerusalem, but also an ample donation above and beyond that for the needy church in Jerusalem. The local churches of Europe were not to live hermetically sealed existences apart from the apostolic churches elsewhere in the world. They had to have a catholic vision, a universal embrace of the cause of Christ. They could not dabble in the playground of their own little ministries; they had to stay connected to the big picture, the total ministry of the church in the world. So, Paul appeals to them to be as generous as they can and expresses the foundational thought behind all Christian stewardship. They are not to give because they like the sermon or the preacher, not to earn their own salvation, not to purchase a better seat in the hall, not to show off their wealth, not to purify their own spirits. Why are they to give? "Under the test of this service, you will glorify God by your obedience in acknowledging the gospel of Christ" (2 Corinthians 9:13). If selfishness glorifies the self, then generosity glorifies God. We only give back what we ourselves have received: "Thanks be to God for his inexpressible gift!" (2 Corinthians 9:15).

"My grace is sufficient for you" (2 Corinthians 12:9). Concerned that the Corinthians may feel overwhelmed by the demands he is placing upon them, Paul commends them to trust in God and His provident care. When God asks for something, He gives the means to fulfill what is requested. Every call is also a gift. Nothing is impossible for God, and therefore God can give, miraculously if necessary, all the support and strength needed to perform any tasks for Him. Paul himself is in the very midst of performing amazing feats for God, and invites the Corinthians and us to do wonders by God's power rather than our own. Remember Paul's fundamental teaching from the First Letter to the Corinthians—the power of the Cross. If Christ could save the world by means of His suffering, then surely His followers can do the little this or that required here and there in response. Golden moments lie in wait when the time is right, to advance the kingdom of God, maybe lighting just one candle to pierce the darkness. Grace is ready for us at every turning point. Are we ready for grace?

"Here for the third time I am ready to come to you" (2 Corinthians 12:14). Finally, in the Fall of the year AD 57, Paul actually returns to his beloved Corinth. He finds the community intact and ready for him and spends about half a year there. Since the death of the Emperor Claudius in October of year AD 54, most of the Roman exiles who had lived among the Corinthians have returned to Rome and are in the process of rebuilding their community life. Paul in Ephesos remembered Corinth, but Paul in Corinth imagines Rome and conceives a powerful desire to go there (Acts 19:21). During his second stay in Corinth, Paul writes his masterpiece, the Letter to the Romans. Unlike his other letters, written back to communities he had already visited, this letter introduces him to a city he had never seen. He knows people there, his adopted Paullus relatives are there, and he has a good sense of the problems and opportunities awaiting him there. Corinth for Paul is now, and perhaps always has been, a stepping-stone to Rome. Before Paul can reach his Roman destiny, however, he must return to Jerusalem to be put in chains.

Christ and the Church

Paul was at the same time converted to Christ and to the Church. This leads one to understand why the Church later became so present in Paul's thoughts, heart and activity. … When he spoke of his "anxiety for all the churches" (2 Corinthians 11:28), he was thinking of the various Christian communities brought into being from time to time in Galatia, Ionia, Macedonia, and in Achaea. … He felt bound to the Communities he founded in a way that was far from cold and bureaucratic but rather intense and passionate. Thus, for example, he described the Philippians as "my brethren, whom I love and long for, my joy and my crown" (Philippians 4:1).

… Let us pray to the Lord to be like this, in communion with Christ and in communion with ourselves.

Pope Benedict XVI, *General Audience* (November 22, 2006)

---

1. Read 2 Corinthians and choose your favorite verse.

2. Identify the main idea in the following passages.

2 Corinthians 1:3–5	
2 Corinthians 1:6–7	
2 Corinthians 1:11	
2 Corinthians 1:12–14	
2 Corinthians 1:24	

3. What can you learn from the following?

Sirach 23:9	
Matthew 5:34–37	
2 Corinthians 1:17–24	
James 5:12	
CCC 1065	

* How can your speech become more straightforward and loving? Do you give in to excessive flattery? Do you see the negative rather than the positive? Do you whine and complain about your lot in life? Do you nag or criticize others? Do you make empty promises and then not keep your word? What could you do to improve your speech and make it more pleasing to God?

4. What enables you to spread the aroma of Christ?

2 Corinthians 2:14–16	
Sirach 24:15	
CCC 1294	

5. What can you learn from the following passages?

Exodus 34:33–35	
2 Corinthians 3:12–16	
CCC 702	
2 Corinthians 3:17–18	

6. To what ministry is Paul called? 2 Corinthians 4:1–12

7. What faith and hope do you have from Christ?

2 Corinthians 4:13–18	
CCC 989	

8. Find and explain the truths contained in the following passage.

2 Corinthians 5:1–10	
CCC 1005	
CCC 1021	
CCC 1681	

9. Describe yourself from these verses.

2 Corinthians 5:17	
2 Corinthians 5:20	

* When were you an ambassador for Christ? What kind of ambassador are you?

10. What time is it?

2 Corinthians 6:1–3	
CCC 1041	

11. Give a practical example of 2 Corinthians 6:14–16.

12. What can confrontation of sin and godly grief produce? 2 Corinthians 7:8–12

13. Identify some principles in the following passages.

Exodus 16:17–18	
Proverbs 11:24–25	
Psalm 112:9	
2 Corinthians 8:1–16	
CCC 2833	
2 Corinthians 9:6–15	

* In what ways are you generous with you time, talent, and treasure?

14. Find some practical wisdom in these verses.

2 Corinthians 10:5	
2 Corinthians 10:17	
2 Corinthians 10:18	

15. How can you hold your thoughts captive to Christ? 1 Thessalonians 5:16–18

16. Find a concern and a warning in these verses.

2 Corinthians 11:2–4	
2 Corinthians 11:13–15	

17. Explain the drama in 2 Corinthians 12:2–7.

18. Use the Catechism to explain 2 Corinthians 12:9–10.

2 Corinthians 12:9–10	
CCC 268	
CCC 273	
CCC 1508	

19. What can you proclaim about the power of God?

2 Corinthians 13:3–4	
CCC 648	

20. How should Christians live in the world? 2 Corinthians 13:11–14

Chapter 16

God's Righteousness
Romans 1–4

**For I am not ashamed of the gospel: it is the power of God for salvation
to every one who has faith, to the Jew first and also to the Greek.
For in it the righteousness of God is revealed through faith for faith;
as it is written, "He who through faith is righteous shall live."**
Romans 1:16–17

The Letter of Paul to the Romans, the longest of the Pauline letters, was written around the year AD 57, while he was ministering to the church in Corinth (Romans 15:25–28, 1 Corinthians 16:3–5). Paul wanted to bring a contribution for the poor and suffering Christians in Jerusalem, and then move on to visit the city of Rome, before embarking on a missionary journey to Spain.

Paul writes to the Christians in Rome—some are Jews and others are Gentiles. Paul presupposes that the readers of this letter who are Jews are familiar with the Hebrew Scriptures. He also uses some methods of argumentation that were common among Jews and Greeks of his day. Paul raises a proposition and then presents some arguments for and against that proposition, before coming to a final resolution. At times, Paul seems to be addressing an imaginary person who might pose certain objections. Cognizant of this style of developing an argument with the intention of proclaiming a spiritual truth, it is imperative to read a large section of scripture in one sitting. Taking one verse out of context is very dangerous, as it can give the reader a wrong understanding, very different from what Paul intended. Hence, the layperson should proceed prayerfully and cautiously under the guidance of the Holy Spirit, always submitting to the teaching authority of the Church, the Magisterium.

The primary thrust of the first part of Romans is to establish the absolute righteousness of God, in contrast to man's weakness and sinfulness. At this point in the history of the Jewish people, some Jews assumed that belonging to God's Chosen People, circumcised under Mosaic Law, ensured that they were set apart from the rest of men, and ready for their heavenly reward. In the city of Rome, Judaizing missionaries wanted Gentiles to be circumcised as well as baptized.

No rabbi of Paul's day ever taught that Gentiles would have to be circumcised in order to be saved. Why should the church demand circumcision of God-fearing non-Jews, when even the synagogue did not demand it? Jesus never asked the apostles to circumcise anyone. Instead, Jesus said, "Go therefore and make disciples of all nations, baptizing them in the name of the Father and of the Son and of the Holy Spirit" (Matthew 28:19). So the Judaizers succeeded in misrepresenting both Judaism and Christianity, distorting the authentic teaching of both religions.

Circumcision was the first law observed by a Jew, on the eighth day after his birth, bringing him under the jurisdiction of the 613 laws of the Mosaic code. However, rabbis do not consider circumcision to be the greatest of the commandments. The Torah speaks of mercy (Genesis 19:19), just as the Gospel does. Therefore, when Paul speaks against "the law," he does not mean "the Torah," but rather, an entire mentality of legalism which is by no means limited to Jewish circles. The Romans too had their law, the "Lex Romana," by which they administered their empire. Paul does not want Roman Law to replace Jewish Law, but rather he wants the very idea of law to be transcended by adherence to gospel values of mercy.

Paul attempted to level the playing field between the Jews and the Gentiles. Belonging to Israel, the Chosen People of God, is a special privilege with major responsibilities. Because the Jews have received the revelation of God, the divine light, they have a responsibility to share the truth of God with the world. The Jews of Paul's time may have had a "them and us" attitude. Jews are special, the redeemed of the Lord, and non-Jews are outsiders, sinners, the lost. Paul uses shocking language to try to shake up the Jews from their complacency. God's wrath will come upon all wickedness (Romans 1:18). Here Paul is careful to show that sinful behavior will warrant punishment by any person who resists the truth, Jew or Gentile. The point is to show that God is impartial and a just judge.

God's divine mercy and impartiality responds to man's repentance. God does not exercise justice by relying on external appearances or specific categories such as circumcision or non-circumcision, but rather God looks at the motive and considers the sincere attitude of the heart and the faithful obedience to His Will, in judging each person. God sees the heart, which man cannot see or judge.

> The compassion of man is for his neighbor,
> but the compassion of the Lord is for all living beings.
> He rebukes and trains and teaches them,
> and turns them back, as a shepherd his flock.
> He has compassion on those who accept his discipline
> and who are eager for his judgments.
>
> Sirach 18:13–14

Paul confronts the hypocrisy of those who judge the sinful behavior of unbelievers while remaining oblivious to their own personal wrongdoing. God's kindness and mercy are intended to lead each person to genuine repentance, not just those sinners out there among the pagans. Jews and non-Jews alike will be punished for personal sins and rewarded for obedience and good deeds.

You can fool some of the people some of the time, but you can't fool God. God is perfect in mercy and justice. God will judge every person according to his works (Romans 2:6). This concept was already revealed in the Old Testament.

> If you say, "Behold, we did not know this,"
>   does not he who weighs the heart perceive it?
> Does not he who keeps watch over your soul know it,
>   and will he not repay man according to his work?
>
> Proverbs 24:12

People may try to convince themselves that because they are no longer sinners, but members of the family of God, they are entitled to cut a few corners, take a few privileges, or indulge a few passions of the flesh. Perhaps God will overlook unfair business practices or stealing from others if a contribution is made at the altar? Or, perhaps if no one knows about this gossip, this affair, this abortion, it won't be an issue. First century people may have been quite similar to some contemporary Christians. Paul tries to shake them out of their complacency, and the Holy Spirit may intend to wake up modern day believers from their complacency as well.

A matter of the heart must be considered. God desires a pure heart and obedience to His commands. Hypocrisy and outward demonstrations of piety cannot cover over hidden grave sins—bitterness, resentment, envy, unforgiveness, and the like.

> I the Lord search the mind
>   and try the heart,
>   to give to every man according to his ways,
>   according to the fruit of his doings.
>
> Jeremiah 17:10

Perhaps these strong words of Paul would have prompted people to examine their consciences and return to God. "Search me, O God, and know my heart! Try me and know my thoughts! And see if there be any wicked way in me, and lead me in the way everlasting!" (Psalm 139:23–24).

The sharp words of Paul were intended to rouse the people to action. God is rich in mercy and justice to all, Jew and non-Jew alike. And God will judge all, Jews and Gentiles according to the purity of their hearts and the fruit of their works. Paul says clearly in Romans that God "will render to every man according to his works" (Romans 2:6). So, faith in God and obedience are both essential responses to God. Paul insists that the believer needs "faith working through love" (Galatians 5:6). Saint James expounds on this point by saying that "faith by itself, if it has no works, is dead" (James 2:17). Charity is the natural outgrowth of genuine faith.

Paul exposes the universality of evil. The presence of evil in the world in each and every generation and culture is obvious to all. Paul wants to again level the playing field by shocking the Jewish and Gentile Christian readers to consider the truth of the Old Testament revelation that wickedness is prevalent in our world.

> The fool says in his heart, "There is no God."
>> They are corrupt, they do abominable deeds,
>> there is none that does good.
> The Lord looks down from heaven upon the children of men,
>> to see if there are any that act wisely, that seek after God.
> They have all gone astray, they are all alike corrupt;
>> there is none that does good, no, not one.
>
> Psalm 14:1–3

Paul assembles a catena (chain) of quotations from six different psalms (Romans 3–18) to hammer home the depravity of the unredeemed universe. Fools continue to attest that there is no God, or that God will not care about what people do. In fact, God has cared, and has continued to intervene with His grace, especially since sending His Son into the world to redeem it.

"All have sinned and fall short of the glory of God, they are justified by his grace as a gift" (Romans 3:23–24). There are two ways to examine the above verse. The distributive sense attests that each and every human being has sinned. This cannot be a true interpretation. First, the Bible tells us that Jesus never sinned (Hebrews 4:15). The Bible cannot contradict itself, so the distributive sense cannot fit. Logically, the baby who dies in infancy is incapable of sinning, because he cannot make a willful decision to sin. Sin is a grave offense against God that is committed with full knowledge and complete consent of the will. A person must freely choose to act against God, which an infant, and some handicapped adults, are incapable of doing. Therefore, the literal, distributive sense of this Bible passage does not work.

Another approach uses the collective sense in interpreting this passage. Paul uses the collective approach here to show that Jews and Gentiles fall into sin. Paul's language here could be similar to contemporary patterns of speech. "Everyone likes chocolate" does not mean that each and every person on the earth likes chocolate. It is a truism that most people, adults and children, indeed do, enjoy chocolate.

> In making man in his image and likeness, God "crowned him with glory and honor," but by sinning, man fell "short of the glory of God." From that time on, God was to manifest his holiness by revealing and giving his name, in order to restore man to the image of his creator.
>
> CCC 2809

Another exception to the literal sense of Romans 3:23–24 is the Blessed Virgin Mary. Mary was born without original sin and remained sinless throughout her earthly life, by God's grace. God cannot exist in the presence of sin. Therefore, it is fitting that Jesus would be born from the womb of a pure and sinless vessel. Once again, logic and reason support the true biblical understanding of texts.

The Doctrine of the Immaculate Conception

The most Blessed Virgin Mary was, from the first moment of her conception, by a singular grace and privilege of Almighty God and by virtue of the merits of Jesus Christ, preserved from all stain of original sin.

Pope Pius IX, *Ineffabilis Deus* (1854)

Mary received God's grace from the moment of her conception. She chose to remain in God's grace throughout her life on earth. You can receive God's grace in the faith He gives so graciously to each person. Repent of your sin and thank God for the precious gift of faith. Then, frequent the sacraments to receive more faith and more grace to be obedient to God.

* Read the Letter to the Romans in one sitting and choose your favorite verse.

1. How does the writer of this letter identify himself? Romans 1:1–6

2. What is Paul's objective? Romans 1:7–14

3. Compare the following verses.

Habakkuk 2:4	
Romans 1:16–17	
Galatians 3:11–12	
Philippians 3:8–9	
Hebrews 10:38–39	

4. Can someone who hasn't heard the Gospel know God?

Romans 1:18–28	
CCC 32	
CCC 1777	

* Who shared God's good news with you?

5. Compare the following lists of sins and the result of these sins.

Romans 1:29–32	
Galatians 5:19–21	
Ephesians 5:3–5	
CCC 1852	

6. What is described in these passages? Romans 2:1–3, 17–24

7. God's mercy is meant to lead the sinner to what? Romans 2:4

8. To what do the following passages point?

Romans 2:25–29	
Deuteronomy 30:6	
Jeremiah 4:1–4	

9. What special advantage do Jews enjoy? Romans 3:1–8

10. Compare the following passages.

Psalm 14:1–3	
Isaiah 59:7–8	
Romans 3:9–23	

11. Find a solution to the sin problem.

Romans 1:16–17, 3:22	
Ephesians 1:7–10	
Colossians 1:11–14	
Hebrews 9:15	

12. How and when was Abraham justified? Romans 4:1–12

13. On whom does David pronounce a blessing? Romans 4:6–8, Psalm 32:1–2

14. How will all nations be blessed through Abraham's progeny? CCC 706

15. What does the fulfillment of God's promise require? Romans 4:13–16

16. Who are the true descendants of Abraham? Romans 4:13–25

17. What was Abraham's attitude? Romans 4:20–21

18. How is Abraham similar to God the Father? CCC 2572

19. How can righteousness be reckoned to you? Romans 4:22–25

20. What can help you deal with the sin problem in your own life? CCC 1460

* When was the last time you went to Confession? Could you go this week?

Monthly Social Activity

This month, your small group will meet for coffee, tea, or a simple breakfast, lunch, or dessert in someone's home. Pray for this social event and for the host or hostess. Try, if at all possible, to attend.

After a short prayer and some time for small talk, write down a difficult situation that God was able to redeem or turn to good. Try to share about this situation in a five-minute time frame.

Examples:

◆ *I couldn't afford to go to college right out of high school. So, I took a job that turned out to be very satisfying. Later, my employer told me about a tuition reimbursement program that allowed me to go to night school, at a time when I was much more mature.*

◆ *My father's job required several moves. Although it was difficult to leave friends and go to a new school, I made many friends and learned to be flexible and willing to change.*

◆ *My grandparents spoke very little English. Listening to them and speaking with them, I became proficient in two languages.*

Chapter 17

Response to Grace
Romans 5–8

**Therefore, since we are justified by faith,
we have peace with God through our Lord Jesus Christ.**
Romans 5:1

In the beginning of Paul's letter to the Romans, he uses very strong words and exaggerations, in an attempt to get his readers to recognize their sinfulness and need for God. He contrasts the perfect holiness and justice of God against the wickedness of humanity. That Paul's words are not meant to be taken literally, can be seen by looking at the many scripture passages that contradict them. "No one seeks for God" (Romans 3:11) sounds similar to "God looks down from heaven upon the sons of men to see if there are any … that seek after God" (Psalm 53:2). Obviously, literally there *are* people who seek God. Moses invited everyone who sought the Lord to go to the meeting tent (Exodus 33:7). Uzziah sought the Lord (2 Chronicles 26:5). David sought the Lord. "I sought the Lord, and he answered me, and delivered me from all my fears (Psalm 34:4). Zacchaeus sought the Lord. Paul sought the Lord. You are seeking the Lord.

Paul's strong language and exaggerations are intended to place his readers in a humble posture. They must recognize their need for salvation before they can accept the Savior that God sends. The contemporary situation may be similar to the one Paul faced. Many people think that they aren't so bad. They are nice people. They go to church. They don't want to get too carried away with this religious business. Do you understand how desperately you need Jesus? It can be hard for nice people to see their need for a Redeemer. God has provided the solution to the sin problem in the free and gracious gift of His Son, Our Lord Jesus Christ.

> Love is so much the gift of God that it is called God. Let no one say to himself: "If [justification] is from faith, how is it freely given: If faith merits it, why is it not rather paid than given?" Let the faithful man not say such a thing: for, if he says: "I have faith, therefore I merit justification," he will be answered: "What have you that you have not received?" If, therefore, faith entreats and receives justification, according as God has apportioned to each in the measure of his faith, nothing of human merit precedes the grace of God, but grace itself merits increase, and the increase merits perfection, with the will accompanying but not leading, following along but not going in advance.
>
> Saint Augustine of Hippo (354–430 AD)
> *Letter of Augustine to Paulinus of Nola, 186, 3, 7–10*

Recognizing one's sinfulness and need for God, the humble person looks to God for redemption. God's love offers salvation to those who are justified by faith. After repentance and baptism, the Christian is invited into the family of God and experiences a peace that surpasses the trials and tribulations of life. God's love is so profound and beyond human understanding that God showed His love by sending Jesus to die for the sins of the world, even while the world was still in sin. God did not wait for repentance to provide this sovereign act of divine grace and mercy.

> When we are baptized, we are enlightened. Being enlightened, we are adopted as sons. Adopted as sons, we are made perfect. Made perfect, we are become immortal. This work is variously called grace, illumination, perfection, and washing. It is a washing by which we are cleansed of sins; a gift of grace by which the punishments due our sins are remitted; an illumination by which we behold that holy light of salvation—that is, by which we see God clearly; and we call that perfection which leaves nothing lacking. Indeed, if a man know God, what more does he need? Certainly it was out of place to call that which is not complete a true gift of God's grace. Because God is perfect, the gifts He bestows are perfect.
> Saint Clement of Alexandria (150–216 AD) *Paidagogos*, 1, 6, 26, 1

After having focused previously on divine justice, Paul now moves to the concept of divine grace. Perhaps it would be best to think of justification and salvation in terms of a process, rather than a one–time event. Jesus Christ redeemed us from the penalty of our sins on Calvary. Repentance and baptism bring the believer into the family of God and the work of sanctification begins. The old man dies with Christ in the waters of baptism and a new creature emerges. Death—physical death and spiritual death—no longer has power over him. And yet, sin and temptation remain. Paul assures the believer that "sin will have no dominion over you" (Romans 6:14) because of God's grace.

Despite the goodness of the law, without grace it is impossible to obey God. The interior conflict between good and evil persists. Some people presume that "all you need to do is accept Jesus as your personal Lord and Savior, and your salvation is assured." It is a simple decision, a one-time event. But, Paul's letter to the Romans presents an entirely different scenario. Paul struggles with his flesh, his carnal desires. He wants to be obedient to God and do the right thing, but alas, he fails. "For I do not do the good I want, but the evil I do not want is what I do" (Romans 7:19). The Roman poet Ovid pronounced a similar sentiment, "I perceive what is better and approve of it, but I pursue what is worse." The spiritual life is a continual battle.

Most honest Christians could identify with such a struggle. The alcoholic must decide for sobriety every single day. The gossip wants to speak charitably, but falls and must repent. The wealthy person wants to help the poor but passes by the beggar instead. The glutton ignores the diet and hides forbidden sweets from others in the household. How many Catholics become discouraged, needing to confess the same sins in Confession, time and time again? Rather than becoming discouraged, Paul provides hope and practical assistance for weak believers. Santification is a process.

"There is therefore now no condemnation for those who are in Christ Jesus" (Romans 8:1). Even though sinful people deserve condemnation, Jesus rescues people from enslavement to sin and makes it possible for them to live according to the Holy Spirit. In baptism, the Holy Spirit is given, indeed indwells the believer. A greater outpouring of the Holy Spirit is received in the Sacrament of Confirmation. The power of the Holy Spirit enables the Christian to rise above sin and maintain fellowship with God. The Holy Spirit is the life-giving power of God Himself. The word "Spirit" occurs five times in Romans 1–7, but Paul mentions "Spirit" 29 times in Romans chapter 8. The Holy Spirit enables the person to find reconciliation and peace with God. Through the Spirit, the Christian becomes a child of God and can call God "Abba" Father, just as Jesus does (Romans 8:15). Only Jesus can bring a sinner home and makes him part of the family.

> The Holy Spirit is the gift that comes into man's heart together *with prayer*. In prayer he manifests himself first of all and above all as the gift that "helps us in our weakness. …" The Holy Spirit not only enables us to pray, but guides us "from within" in prayer: he is present in our prayer and gives it a divine dimension. Thus *"he who searches the hearts of men knows what is the mind of the Spirit,* because the Spirit intercedes for the saints according to the will of God."* Prayer through the power of the Holy Spirit becomes the ever more mature expression of the new man, who by means of this prayer participates in the divine life.
>
> *Our difficult age has a special need of prayer.* … So, too, recent years have been seeing a growth in the number of people who, in ever more widespread movements and groups, are giving first place to prayer and seeking in prayer a renewal of their spiritual life. This is a significant and comforting sign, for from this experience there is coming a real contribution to the revival of prayer among the faithful, who have been helped to gain a clearer idea of the Holy Spirit as he who inspired in hearts a profound yearning for holiness.
>
> Pope John Paul II, *Dominum et Vivificantem* (May 18, 1986) 65.2–3)

The way to conquer sin and death is to repent and accept the free grace of God, given in Jesus. The Holy Spirit then draws the believer up into a life of prayer. God initiates the process of justification and sanctification in love through grace. The believer is responsible to respond to the free gift of God by receiving or rejecting it. Grace and power are available through the sacraments.

So, now having identified the problem of sin and wickedness, Paul shows the Christian how to live a life of freedom from sin, by the power of the Holy Spirit. When the Christian is living in the life of the Spirit, he experiences the peace of God. Even suffering is bearable and produces character, endurance, and hope. Furthermore, Paul assures the believer that if we have died with Christ, we will be united with Him in a resurrection like His (Romans 6:5). So, thanks to Jesus' Resurrection from the dead and the gift of baptism, the Christian anticipates the resurrection of his body in the world to come. Along the path of this earthly pilgrimage to heaven, the Holy Spirit helps the believer throughout his life, and gives personal guidance and direction.

The Holy Spirit makes us sons and daughter of God. He involves us in the same responsibility that God has for his world, for the whole of humanity. He teaches us to look at the world, others and ourselves with God's eyes. We do not do good as slaves who are not free to act otherwise, but we do [good] because we are personally responsible for the world; because we love truth and goodness, because we love God himself and therefore, also his creatures. This is the true freedom to which the Holy Spirit wants to lead us.

We want the true, great freedom, the freedom of heirs, the freedom of children of God. In this world, so full of fictitious forms of freedom that destroy the environment and the human being, let us learn true freedom by the power of the Holy Spirit; to build the school of freedom; to show others by our lives that we are free and how beautiful it is to be truly free with the freedom of God's children.

The Holy Spirit, in giving life and freedom, also gives unity. To understand it, we might find a sentence useful which at first seems rather to distance us from it. Jesus said to Nicodemus, who came to him with his questions by night: "The wind blows where it wills" (John 3:8). But, the Spirit's will is not arbitrary. It is the will of truth and goodness. Therefore, he does not blow from anywhere, now from one place and then from another; his breath is not wasted but brings us together because the truth unites and love unites.

The Holy Spirit is the Spirit of Jesus Christ, the Spirit who unites the Father with the Son in Love, which in the one God he gives and receives. He unites us so closely that Saint Paul once said: "You are all one in Jesus Christ" (Galatians 3:28).

Pope Benedict XVI, *Vigil of Pentecost Homily* (June 3, 2006)

This year, renew your baptismal promises with great fervor at Easter. Ask God to give you a greater outpouring of the Holy Spirit. Live in the light. Find a trusted friend or spiritual director who will hold you accountable in your struggles with sin and temptation. Be docile to the Holy Spirit in prayer, confident that God is making you into a child of the family, into a SAINT!

1. How and when did God save mankind?

Romans 5:1–11	
CCC 604	

2. What good is suffering? Romans 5:3–5

3. Why would Paul contrast the example of Christ with the sin of Adam?

Romans 5:12–19	
CCC 388	

4. What can you learn about "grace" from Romans 5?

5. How can you be justified?

Romans 5:1–2, 5	
Romans 6:1–14	
CCC 1987	

6. What will "yielding to righteousness" produce? Romans 6:19

7. Compare two types of slavery.

Slaves of _____	Slaves of GOD
Romans 6:16	Romans 6:17–19
Romans 6:20–21	Romans 6:22
Romans 6:23	Romans 6:23

8. What is the free gift of God? Romans 6:23

9. What can you say about death?

Romans 6:1–4, 23	
CCC 1006	
CCC 1008	

10. Is the law good or bad? Romans 7:1–12, CCC 1963

11. Compare the following passages.

Romans 6:20–23	Romans 7:5–6

12. Describe the conflict in Romans 7:14–23.

13. Compare the following verses.

Romans 7:15	
Galatians 5:17	

* How have you felt inner conflict over trying to conform better to God's law?

14. What good news can you find in these passages?

Romans 5:16	
Romans 8:1	

15. What hope and direction can you find in the following verses?

Romans 8:9–11	
1 Corinthians 3:16, 6:19	
2 Timothy 1:13–14	

16. What Christian truth can you anticipate from this verse?

Romans 8:11	
CCC 989	

17. What does the Holy Spirit give you? * How can you get more of the Spirit?

Romans 8:14	
Romans 8:15–18	
Romans 8:26–27	

18. What is the condition of the world (creation)? Romans 8:19–23

19. Proclaim the good news found in Romans 8:28.

20. Write your favorite verse from Romans 8:31–39. Memorize it this week!

Chapter 18

God's Universal Plan
Romans 9–16

**None of us lives to himself, and none of us dies to himself.
If we live, we live to the Lord, and if we die, we die to the Lord;
so then, whether we live or whether we die, we are the Lord's.
For to this end Christ died and lived again,
that he might be Lord both of the dead and the living.**
Romans 14:7–9

Rome was the hub or center of the known world in the First Century AD. Rome was comparable to New York City in contemporary times. So, if you can make it in New York, you can succeed anywhere. Paul knows that if the Christian message can flourish in Rome, the Gospel will advance throughout the entire world. Rome held critical importance for Christendom in Paul's day, as it does today!

Throughout the Letter to the Romans, Paul uses a type of shorthand. He mentions a name or a phrase from the Hebrew Scriptures, assuming that his readers will connect with the full story. If today you mentioned Abraham Lincoln, you could assume that people would recall where he was from, how he lived, his famous Gettysburg Address, his major contributions to society, and the way in which he died. Similarly, when Paul mentions Adam, Abraham, Moses, Pharaoh, Jacob, Esau, Isaiah, and others, he presupposes that the reader is familiar with the entire passages containing those names. For the unfamiliar, it will require researching the Old Testament text and reading the larger context in full.

Paul begins this part of Romans by recalling God's election of the Jews, His Chosen People. He hopes that many more Jews will accept God's mercy by believing in Jesus Christ. Throughout this letter, Paul uses the terms "circumcision" and "works" almost interchangeably to refer to circumcision and the ceremonial rituals of animal sacrifice, which were part of the Mosaic Law. He uses exaggerated language to try to shake people out of their complacency, believing that merely being circumcised, obeying Kosher dietary laws, and offering sacrifices would be enough to ensure a place in heaven. Paul recognizes that the Jews are God's elect, His Chosen People, and they must also be a people of faith and obedience.

"Not from the Jews only but also from the Gentiles" (Romans 9:24). Paul is concerned with the role of non-Jewish people in God's plan also. On several occasions he has already said "to the Jews first and also the Greeks" (Romans 1:6, 2:9, 2:10; see 3:9 and 3:29). The "Romans" to whom he wrote were immigrant Greeks and Greek-speaking Jews, as well as native Romans, many of whom as educated people also knew Greek. The language of the Christian community in Rome was Greek in Paul's time, and the Roman liturgy was celebrated in Greek until the Fourth Century. Rome had political power, Greeks had intellectual power, but Hebrews had spiritual power, and Paul strives to bind them all together into one commonwealth of faith.

> It is not a question of him who wills nor of him who runs, but of God's showing mercy. ... There are some people who are so proud of their successes that they attribute everything to themselves and nothing to Him who made them and gave them wisdom and supplied them with good things. Let them learn of this saying that even to wish someone well requires God's help; or rather, that even to choose what is right is something divine and a gift of God's benevolence to man. That we be saved requires something from us and from God. That is why it says 'Not of him who wills;' that is, not *only* of him who wills; and not *only* of him who runs, but *also* of God's mercy. Since to will is also from God, it is reasonable that Paul attributed the whole to God. However well you may run, however well you may wrestle, you still need Him who gives the crown.
> Saint Gregory Nazianzen (330–389 AD) *On the Gospel of Matthew,* 37:13

Jewish Christians and Gentile Christians attribute every good gift, including the gift of faith, as a precious, undeserved gift from Almighty God. Pride presents a tremendous danger in wrongly assuming that the believer has earned something meritorious by virtue of the response freely given to God's profound gift. The focus should be on God, the one who chooses and the One who gives the gift of faith and the grace to respond to the gift, rather than on the believer.

> Everything depends on God, but not so as to hinder our free will. "But if it depends on God," someone will say, "Why does He blame us?" That is why I said, "Not so as to hinder our free will." It depends upon us and upon Him. We first must choose the good, and when we have chosen, then does He provide that which is His part. He does not anticipate our choice, lest violence be done to our free will. But when we have chosen, then great is the assistance He provides us. ... Our part is to choose and to will; God's part is to perfect and to bring to an end. Since, then, the greater part is God's, [Paul] speaks after the fashion of men and says that the whole of it is God's. For example, we see a house well built, and we say that it is all due to the architect; but certainly it is not all due to him, but also to the workmen, the owner, and many others. Yet, because the architect contributed the greater part, we say that it is all his doing.
>
> Even should you run, even should you strive earnestly, he says, do not suppose that the good result is yours. For if you had not crucial help from above, all were in vain. It is perfectly clear, however, that with that help you will achieve what you earnestly strive for, so long as you also run, and so long as you will it.
> Saint John Chrysostom (344–407 AD), *Homilies on Hebrews,* 12:3–5

Saint Paul and the early Church Fathers attempt to teach the truth of divine election alongside the doctrine of free will. God loves all people. God desires all people to come to Him for salvation. He shows divine mercy and justice. God first revealed Himself to the Jewish people, His Chosen People. Jesus was a Jew. All of the apostles were Jews. Paul himself is a Jew, trained by the most famous rabbi of his time, the Rabbi Gamaliel. Paul, the apostle to the Gentiles, also wants all of the Jews to come to believe in Jesus Christ. Paul reveals that Israel's temporary rejection of Christ will be used by God to extend His mercy to the Gentiles. And, before the Lord comes again, His mercy will be poured out once more upon the Jews.

It was not because we did believe, but so that we might believe, that He chose us, so that we could not be said to have chosen Him first. ... "You have not chosen Me, but I have chosen you." We are called, not because we believed, but so that we might believe; and by that calling which is without repentance it is effected and carried through that we should believe.

Not everyone believes who is called. For many are called, but few are chosen: the chosen are those who were not contemptuous of Him who called them, but believed in Him and followed Him, who believed in Him without doubt because they willed to do so. ... Not everyone who is called obeys the call, since it is in the power of his will not to obey, it can rightly be said that it is not of God who has mercy, but of the man who wills and runs, because the mercy of God's calling him does not suffice unless it be followed by the obedience of him who is called.

Saint Augustine of Hippo (354–430 AD)

The Predestination of the Saints, 19:38, and *Questions to Simplician,* 1:2, 10, 13

Paul's hope is that both Jews and Gentiles will be saved through God's divine mercy. Paul understands that the complete fulfillment of the law has been achieved by the ultimate sacrifice of Jesus Christ on the cross. He ends his discourse with a beautiful hymn to God, found at the conclusion of Romans 11.

O the depth of the riches and wisdom and knowledge of God!
How unsearchable are his judgments and how inscrutable his ways!
"For who has known the mind of the Lord,
or who has been his counselor?"
"Or who has given a gift to him that he might be repaid?"
For from him and through him and to him are all things.
To him be glory for ever. Amen.
Romans 11:33–36

Following this beautiful hymn, Paul asks the believers to present their bodies as a living sacrifice, holy and acceptable to God in spiritual worship (Romans 12:1). Today, the Catholic can offer himself or herself—body, mind, and soul—to God along with the bread and wine offered to Him in the Offertory of the Mass. Jesus offered His body and blood on the cross to God the Father for the redemption of the world. In the Mass, Jesus gives His body, blood, soul, and divinity to believers around the world who hunger and thirst for Him. There is nothing that a person has to give that has not been given to him or her by God. Almighty God desires simply the free gift of self of the believer, returned in worship to Him. While it is impossible to understand the amazing mercy and love of God, the believer can respond in faith and humility offering the meager gift of self back to God.

Having tasted the mercy and love of God, it is the duty of the Christian to pass on this tremendous gift. Paul was a persecutor of Christians, but he became a great missionary and evangelist. The same call is extended to all believers who want to see their friends, neighbors, and family members embrace God's gift of faith.

> An essential part of the Christian faith is the fact that it is meant to be handed on. It consists of coming to know a message that concerns everyone, because it is the truth and because man cannot be saved without the truth. Therefore, catechesis, the transmission of the faith, has been a central vital function of the Church from the beginning and will necessarily remain one for as long as there is a Church.
> Pope Benedict XVI, *Handing on the Faith in an Age of Disbelief*
> (San Francisco: Ignatius Press, 2006), p. 13

Evangelizing is an act of charity. Considering the severe risks of spending eternity separated from God, one must think more of a brother's need for salvation than of one's own discomfort in sharing the Gospel. Also, several lists of spiritual gifts are given in various letters (1 Corinthians 12:1–12, Ephesians 4:11–12). In Romans, Paul lists seven spiritual gifts used for building up the body of Christ—prophecy, service, teaching, exhortation, generosity, giving aid, and works of mercy.

Love is the nature of God and the essence of the Christian life. Paul encourages the believers to love one another, and to outdo one another in showing honor. "Never flag in zeal, be aglow with the Spirit, serve the Lord" (Romans 12:11). These words have encouraged weary Christians over the centuries. It is hard to continue to love, when love is not reciprocated. The Christian must even show mercy to an enemy who is hungry or in need. The practical admonitions for Christian living are easier to write than to live. Who finds it easy to forgive an enemy, much less show kindness? Christians must be humble, not haughty, looking to other's needs. Paul advises living in harmony and peaceably with all people, insofar as it is possible. These challenges confront Christians today as dramatically as they did the Romans who read this letter almost 2,000 years ago. Judgment is not the prerogative of the believer. Many Christians in the early church chose to fast and pray on Wednesdays and Fridays. Some were not strong enough to fast.

Those who could fast were not to pass judgment on those who could not. The goal is to please God and to serve others first and foremost. So, if your fasting makes another believer uncomfortable, choose a different fast day or fast discreetly.

Finally, Paul orients the believers to the ultimate end. "None of us lives to himself, and none of us dies to himself. If we live, we live to the Lord, and if we die, we die to the Lord; so then, whether we live or whether we die, we are the Lord's" (Romans 14:7–8). Life is short. Eternity is forever. Live in such a way that God will be pleased and will be able to say to you on Judgment Day: "Well done, good and faithful servant. ... enter into the joy of your Master" (Matthew 25:23).

1. Explain Paul's emotion concerning Israel. Romans 9:1–5; 10:1

2. What are the implications of God's election of Israel, God's Chosen People?

Romans 9:6–33	
CCC 674	
Romans 11:1–10	
Romans 11:25–35	

3. Compare the following passages

Hosea 2:23	
Romans 9:25–26	
Isaiah 10:20–23	
Romans 9:27–29	

4. How can a Jew or Gentile attain righteousness? Romans 9:30–32

5. Who is the culmination of the Law and why?

Romans 10:4	
CCC 1977	

6. What does faith demand?

Romans 10:5–13	
CCC 14	

7. How and why does someone receive a call to preach the Gospel?

Romans 10:14–21	
CCC 875	

* How should a layperson participate in sharing the Good News?

8. What can you learn from these passages?

Romans 11:11–24	
CCC 60	

9. Find a common thread in these verses.

Romans 12:1–2	
1 Peter 2:4–5	
Ephesians 4:23; 5:10	
CCC 2031	

10. With the help of God's grace, what must the baptized continue to do?

Romans 12:2	
CCC 2520	

* What practical thing could you do to present your body and mind to God?

11. Why does the Catholic Church have male priests? Romans 12:4, CCC 1142

12. How does Saint Augustine interpret Romans 12:5? CCC 1372

13. List the gifts described in Romans 12:6–8. Circle the gifts you have.

14. Explain Christian hope. Romans 12:12, CCC 1820

15. Describe the marks of a true Christian. Romans 12:9–21

16. Who is in debt? Romans 13:8, CCC 2845

17. What is the high point of Christian prayer? Romans 13:9–10, CCC 2844

18. Put Romans 14:7–10 in your own words. Give a practical example of this.

19. Explain the forms of prayer described in this passage.

Romans 15:5–6	
CCC 2627	

20. Who is praising the Lord in Romans 15:10–12?

* Romans 15:7 says to "welcome one another." How do *you* welcome others?

Galatians
Galatians 1–6

**O foolish Galatians! Who has bewitched you,
before whose eyes Jesus Christ was publicly portrayed as crucified?
Let me ask you only this:
Did you receive the Spirit by works of the law, or by hearing with faith?**
Galatians 3:1–2

About that time Paul wrote ahead to the Romans, whom he planned to visit some day, he also wrote to the Galatians, whom he had already visited. These two letters have a symbiotic relationship with each other, covering the same principal Pauline themes of salvation by grace, as well as having many small personal touches in common. Both communities are grappling with the problem affecting the whole church at the time—whether to circumcise Gentiles who convert to Christianity. Paul's message is the same in both cases, that the church should not demand more of Gentiles than the synagogue does, but it transcends this immediate concern to paint in broad strokes the larger issues at hand. The Letter to the Galatians has been called the Magna Carta of Christian freedom.

On closer inspection, the tone and emphasis does differ from one letter to the other. The two communities are very different. Galatia is a provincial, largely rural province inhabited by unschooled "barbarians" of Gallic descent who barely know Greek and without a large Jewish presence. Rome is a cosmopolitan community where the Gentile converts have had to manage affairs during the six years when the Jewish component of the community had been in exile and where most of the Jews and pagans speak Greek fluently. The "Romans" probably did not have to translate their letter into Latin for it to be understood, but the "Galatians" most likely needed a translator for their letter. Recall Paul's visit on the first journey to nearby Lystra, when the local people acclaimed Barnabas and Paul as gods in the own language (Acts 14:11).

Today, little is known about the "churches of Galatia" (Galatians 1:2). Galatia proper had only two major cities, Ancyra and Pessinus, both far to the north of Paul's zone of activity, and hardly anyone there spoke Greek, the language of the letter. Southern Galatia was more Hellenized and closer to the old Persian road that linked the coast of Asia Minor with the Near East. Probably Paul sent his letter to the communities that lay along that roadway. Some of the people along that road lived in tents and may have been his customers during the decade when he supported himself by tent-making in Tarsus.

Galatia in Acts — On the first missionary journey in the Summer of AD 50, Paul and Barnabas visited Iconium, Lystra, and Derbe (Acts 14), which were technically in the district of Lycaonia but were often called "Southern Galatia." The boundaries of the old Kingdom of Galatia had embraced more territory than the eventual Roman Province of Galatia. The local people were loyal to Roman rule, but rural people are especially traditional in their ways, and old names die hard.

On the second missionary journey in the Spring of 54 AD, Paul recruited the half-Jew Timothy in Lystra, and so the term "Galatian" could be used to describe Timothy. Hence, the two "Letters to Timothy" could be subtitled "Letters to a Galatian." Timothy accompanied Paul and Silas into Phrygia and Galatia (Acts 16:6), where Timothy, as a local boy, could have introduced Paul to Galatians whom he knew. The Galatian Timothy served as Paul's letter of introduction to Galatia, just as the Cypriot Barnabas had been his letter of recommendation to Cyprus on the first journey.

On the third missionary journey, Paul went back to Phrygia and Galatia, both at the beginning of the journey in Spring AD 54 (Acts 18:23), and again at the end of the journey in April, AD 58 (Acts 20:1–6). Paul was definitely following the Persian royal road and made only short visits to the Galatians along the way, not spending much time with them. During the long third journey, while he was at Corinth in the Fall of 57 AD, Paul wrote the Letters to the Romans and the Galatians. Sandwiched between two short visits to Galatia, the Letter to the Galatians gives an excellent picture of the nature of Paul's preaching to those communities at that time.

Contemporary scholarship uses the letters to learn things about the communities, sometimes giving the impression that the author's mind was less important than his readers. In the case of the Corinthians and others, indeed much can be learned about the church from Paul's letter. Other letters, such as that to the Ephesians provide less information about the recipients of the letter. Galatians falls largely into the second category. Since he sent very similar letters to Rome and to Galatia, the mind of Paul and the Spirit within that mind are the principal factors shaping those letters. He sees the same spiritual battle going on everywhere in the world, and he senses that the outcome of this battle will be critical for everyone. To Paul, the Romans and Galatians have shared needs, which include a correct understanding of salvation, a clear assent of the will to the conclusions of the Council of Jerusalem, and holding fast to the teachings of the apostles in the power of the Spirit. Paul recognizes that differences exist between these communities, but what they have in common is even more important.

"You have heard of my former life in Judaism" (Galatians 1:13). The Letters to the Galatians and Romans, though highly theological, also reveal more autobiographical information than any of Paul's other letters. Galatians in particular is a major source of personal data and supplements the accounts in Acts with a number of important details. The self-disclosure in Romans is easier to explain, since it is a letter of introduction to a community he has not yet visited. With the Letter to the Galatians, Paul intends something else, to flesh out a friendship that has already been established in person, but where the occasion did not allow him to tell them everything he wanted them to know. So he says, "You have heard," but not, "I have already told you." Indeed Paul has been counting on others to nourish the seed that he has planted, but he seems to have received a report that the Galatians are falling into error. As a result, he writes to shore up the foundation. Clarifying aspects of his own autobiography must be one of his priorities, not because he wishes to glorify himself, but in order to reassert his apostolic authority: "Am I now seeking the favor of men, or of God?" (Galatians 1:10)

"Then after fourteen years I went up again to Jerusalem" (Galatians 2:1). What seems to be merely personal at first grows into an account of the important Council of Jerusalem. The Letter to the Galatians gives both more and less detail than Acts. Here are some events known only from the second chapter of Galatians:

✳ Titus accompanied Paul to the Council, and the apostles did not require him to be circumcised (Galatians 2:1–3).
✳ False brethren secretly spied on the Council (Galatians 2:4).
✳ The apostles asked Paul to remember the poor (Galatians 2:10).
✳ Peter came afterwards to Antioch (Galatians 2:11).
✳ Paul challenged Peter to act in a consistent manner conerning his suspension of kosher law (Galatians 2:12).
✳ Barnabas was influenced by the circumcision party (Galatians 2:13).

"Certain men came from James" (Galatians 2:12). Acts adds many details about the inner council deliberations, which are not found in Galatians, and only Acts reports the formal conclusions of the council concerning the letter dictated by James. Luke paints a more favorable picture of the apostle James than Paul does. For Luke, James is the negotiator, who forges a compromise between the strict circumcision party and the Antiochenes; for Paul, the circumcisers come from James. These accounts are not too difficult to reconcile. Paul, writing in the heat of the moment, takes out his frustration on poor James, but Luke, writing years later with the advantage of hindsight, knows that James was part of the solution and not part of the problem. The Letter of James seems to collide with Paul's Letter to the Galatians on one of the principal theological points.

"He who through faith is righteous shall live" (Galatians 3:11 quoting Habakkuk 2:4). Paul bases his theological reasoning upon this verse from one of the prophets, but otherwise he interlaces this chapter with quotations from the Law. So, while arguing against "law" as a supreme principal, Paul quotes the Torah, the book of highest authority. In chapter three of Galatians, Paul quotes four of the five Books of Moses:

✳ Genesis 12:3, 12:7, 15:6, 18:18, 22:17–18
✳ Exodus 12:40
✳ Leviticus 18:5
✳ Deuteronomy 21:23, and 27:26.

Clearly, then, what Paul means by "law" is not the Jewish Torah as such, but a principle of legalism that can attach itself to any legal tradition, and turn the letter of the law into an instrument for slaying the spirit. Civil law exists for the sake of justice, religious law for the sake of goodness, military law for the sake of good discipline, and none of these laws are supposed to be worshipped for their own sake. Moses never asked the people to worship the Ten Commandments; in fact he broke the tablets of the law because he found them worshipping a false idol, the golden calf. Since the Torah was never meant to be a false god, the Gospel does not annul it. Instead, Paul finds faith in the patriarchs who received the former covenants.

> For all things that, according to the Law, were prior, whether circumcision of the flesh, or the multitude of sacrificial victims, or the observance of the Sabbath, testified to Christ and foretold Christ's grace. And He is the end of the Law, not by annulling but by fulfilling what is signified. For although He is the Author both of the old ways and of the new, still, He changed the sacraments of the prefigured promises, because He fulfilled the promises and put an end to announcements by His coming as the Announced. But in the area of moral precepts, no decrees of the earlier Testament are rejected; rather, in the gospel teaching many of them are augmented, so that the things which give salvation might be more perfect and more lucid than those which promise a Savior.
>
> Pope Saint Leo The Great (440–461 AD) *Sermons, 63, 5*)

"Abraham believed God" (Galatians 3:6). In both the Letter to the Romans and the Letter to the Galatians, Paul bases his treatment of the virtue of faith by considering the person of Abraham and his example of faith. His point of analysis is that Abraham, the father of faith, became the model for all believers, and the law came through Moses 430 years after Abraham (Galatians 3:17, Exodus 12:40). The fact that Abraham believed and was saved without the Mosaic Law demonstrates that faith precedes law metaphysically as well as chronologically.

Notice, however, that the story of Abraham is found in the Book of Genesis, the first of the five books of Moses. When Jews spoke of the Torah, they meant all five books, not just the ones that described the Covenant of Moses. The text of the Torah relates a series of covenants:

* The original covenant with Adam broken by original sin (Genesis 2–3)
* The covenant with all humanity in the person of Noah (Genesis 6–9)
* The covenant with many nations in the person of Abraham (Genesis 12–25)
* The covenant with Moses and the Hebrews (Exodus — Deuteronomy).

Each successive covenant includes fewer and fewer people but imposes more and more obligations. The final covenant between God and man subsists in the single Person of Christ, True God and True Man, an unbreakable covenant because of the union of the two natures in the Second Person of the Blessed Trinity. All the earlier covenants led up to this one, and each covenant is perfected in Christ. Thus, Adam, Noah, Abraham, and Moses all prepared the way for Jesus.

Paul avoids treating Jesus and Moses as polar opposites by going over Moses' head to Abraham and finding that the supremacy of faith was already present in the first patriarch. Even within Abraham's life, the covenant of faith preceded the covenant of circumcision, because Abraham received the promised son, Isaac, some fifteen years before he received the instruction to circumcise him. The gift precedes the obligation. God's gift comes before everything.

"You are no longer a slave but a son" (Galatians 4:7). The sonship of Isaac includes within it the whole Hebrew people. Similarly, Paul reasons, the sonship of Jesus contains within it the whole Christian people. At Baptism each Christian person becomes adopted into Jesus' own relationship with his Father. We become adoptive sons of God the Father, and adoptive brothers and sisters of Christ, hence co-heirs with Him.

During his first missionary journey, the young man Saul met a Roman official named Paullus and from that time bore his name, signifying that he had been adopted into that noble family. Roman patricians and emperors frequently adopted heirs from their extended family or even from outside:

* In his will, Julius Caesar adopted his nephew Octavian in 44 BC.
* Augustus adopted his stepson Tiberius in AD 4.
* Claudius adopted his stepson Nero in AD 50.
* Nerva adopted his fellow Spaniard Trajan in AD 97.
* In his will, Trajan adopted his countryman Hadrian in AD 117.
* Hadrian adopted Antoninus Pius in AD 138.

The Galatians hear what Paul says about our adoption into Christ in light of the fact that, nearly half the time, the rule of the Mediterranean world depended on the Emperor's adoption of an heir.

"Christ has set us free" (Galatians 5:1). Every kind of spiritual slavery vanishes in the face of our adoption into Christ. When a Roman master freed one of his slaves, he would write a deed of "manumission" and, by virtue of that document, the former slave became a free person, with all the rights of citizenship. Sometimes a slave would save enough money to buy his own freedom, and sometimes someone else would buy a slave for the purpose of setting him free. The technical word for this in Roman law was "redemption." The New Testament is our document of liberation and identifies Jesus as our "Redeemer," who paid the price for our freedom. If at the inestimable cost of His own blood our freedom has been bought and paid for, then we have no right to throw it away by voluntarily entering into spiritual slavery again. If Christ has freed us, then we should be truly free! We have freedom of speech to speak truth, freedom of action to do good, and freedom of worship to adore the One True God, and no authority on earth or under the earth has the right to circumvent our freedom to be good and to do good.

1. In what three ways is the Catholic Church apostolic?

Galatians 1:1	
Matthew 28:16–20	
CCC 857	

2. Why did Jesus die?

Galatians 1:3–5	
CCC 2824	

3. What deception confused the Galatians?

Acts 15:1–5	
Galatians 1:6–7	

* Galatians 1:8 refers to a revelation from an angel contrary to the gospel. Find two non-Christian religions that originated from an alleged revelation from an angel to an individual person, giving a message contrary to the gospel. Hint: Look up Mohammed and Joseph Smith.

4. How did Paul receive the gospel?

Galatians 1:10–17	
CCC 442	
Acts 26:4–17	
CCC 659	

5. In what way did Paul speak to the Council of Jerusalem elders? Galatians 2:1–2

6. How did Paul see his mission compared to Peter's mission? Galatians 2:6–10

7. What has always been a major concern of the church? To whom is this concern entrusted?

Galatians 2:10	
CCC 886	

* In what practical ways do you regularly take a concern for the poor and needy?

8. What can you learn from these paragraphs concerning Galatians 2:20?

CCC 478	
CCC 616	
CCC 1380	
CCC 2666	

* How do you experience Christ most personally in your life?

9. Discuss the perfect fulfillment of the law.

Galatians 3:2–12	
CCC 578	
CCC 580	

10. What triumphs over human divisions?

Galatians 3:26–29	
CCC 791	

* List practical ways you can promote unity in the church rather than division.

11. In what ways can you "put on Christ?"

Galatians 3:27	
CCC 1227	
CCC 1425	
CCC 1426	
CCC 2348	

12. What does God provide for humankind?

Galatians 4:1–5	
Galatians 4:6–7	
CCC 683	
CCC 1695	

13. What does it mean to be under the new Law?

Galatians 4:21–31	
CCC 1972	

14. What must we strive for in Christ? Galatians 5:6

_____ *working through* _____

*How can you do this? List some practical ways.

15. Explain Christian freedom.

Galatians 5:1	
CCC 1741	
CCC 1748	

16. Explain fulfillment of the Law.

Leviticus 19:8	
Matthew 22:39	
Galatians 5:14	

17. Paraphrase Galatians 6:7.

18. Contrast works of the flesh and works of the spirit.

Works of the Flesh Galatians 5:19–21	Works of the Spirit Galatians 5:22–23

* Circle the Works of the Spirit are that are most evident in your life right now.

19. How should Christians live?

Galatians 5:25	
Galatians 5:26	
Galatians 6:1	
Galatians 6:2	
Galatians 6:6	
Galatians 6:9	

20. What are you sowing in your life right now? What do you want to sow?

Monthly Social Activity

This month, your small group will meet for coffee, tea, or a simple breakfast, lunch, or dessert in someone's home. Pray for this social event and for the host or hostess. Try, if at all possible, to attend.

After a short prayer and some time for small talk, write down some of the gifts of the Holy Spirit that God is increasing in your life right now.

Then, share about the most memorable thing God taught you in this Bible study.

Finally, write down on a small piece of cardstock the names of three people that you could pray for and invite to Bible study next session.

Examples:

◆ *The Holy Spirit is increasing the gift of joy in my life right now.*

◆ *This year, God taught me that He always has more for me. I can ask Him for more of the Holy Spirit.*

◆ *My sister and my neighbor are two people that I will commit to praying for and then wait on the Holy Spirit for a prompting to ask them to join me at Bible study*

Chapter 20

Appeal to Caesar — AD 60
Acts 20–26

But I do not account my life of any value nor as precious to myself,
if only I may accomplish my course and the ministry
which I received from the Lord Jesus, to testify to the gospel of the grace of God.
Acts 20:24

In May of year 58, Paul concludes his long, third missionary journey by returning to Jerusalem, in the company of the official delegation conveying the temple tax along with donations to the Judean church. Luke gives the names of the delegates—Sopater, Aristarchus, Secundus, Gaius, Timothy, Tychicus and Trophimus (Acts 20:4). The faithful Timothy has won an official place among them, but Silas seems to have disappeared some time in the middle of the third journey.

One other person, left unnamed, has also joined the group, namely Luke, who includes himself in the narrative again by using the first person plural (Acts 20:6). Only once before did he do so, during the second journey, when he accompanied Paul from Troas to Philippi in the year 50 (Acts 16:10–17). Now Luke travels with Paul from Philippi to Jerusalem at the end of the third journey in AD 58. Since Luke puts himself under the radar at Philippi and brings himself back up at Philippi, he seems to imply that he has remained there through the whole eight-year span. If so, then Luke was one of the Philippians to whom Paul wrote his letter.

"After the days of Unleavened Bread" (Acts 20:6) — Paul chose to spend the Passover in Philippi with Luke and the other members of the Christian community there. Needless to say, the opportunity to have the apostle among them for the feast was a great honor for the Philippian church. Luke says that Paul stayed with the God-fearer Lydia on the first visit in the Year 50, and gives no evidence that he stayed elsewhere on his second visit in AD 57, or his third in AD 58. Of course, the Days of Unleavened Bread remind Paul and his fellow Christians of the death and Resurrection of the Lord, which took place in connection with that festival nearly thirty years before. In other words, Paul celebrated Easter in Philippi.

Before Easter, the rest of the delegation already went across the Aegean Sea to Troas, and when the eight Days of Unleavened Bread were completed, Paul and Luke crossed over to join them. The crossing took five days (probably one day of water travel, with two days of land travel on each continent), and the group stayed together in Troas for seven more days.

"On the first day of the week, when we were gathered together to break bread, Paul talked with them" (Acts 20:7). Here we have one of the few indications that during apostolic times, the early church had already moved the Lord's Day from Saturday to

Sunday. The transfer of sabbath rest and worship to Sunday was a sea change even more revolutionary than the suspension of kosher law. The food regulations were secondary legislation, but keeping holy the Sabbath day forms part of the Decalogue. Clearly both changes, and even more the second, required the exercise of the highest authority vested in the apostles and their successors. Scholars normally assert that the generation after the apostles made the change to Sunday, since the New Testament does not contain any open reference to this change. All those scholars should take another look at Acts 20:7. Why is the church of Troas celebrating the breaking of the bread (that is, the Eucharist) on the first day of the week, with one of the apostles physically present to preach at the liturgy? The change must have already taken place in early church communities, thanks to the exercise of the keys entrusted to Peter.

The switch from Saturday to Sunday is understandable in the following way. Jews marked the days from sundown to sundown, so the sabbath day began on Friday evening and continued to the last light on Saturday afternoon. Romans, however, marked the days from sunrise to sunrise. Gentile Christians would begin the sabbath day at sunrise and continue through the night. Jews and Gentiles had days that were twelve hours out of sync with each other. When Luke says that the Troas Christians met on the first day of the week, in the evening, they were meeting on a Saturday night, at a time which Jews no longer considered the sabbath day, but which Gentile Christians would begin to observe as the sabbath. Hence the shift from Friday night (Jewish) to Saturday night (Christian) celebrations was not an act of rebellion against Jewish law but an accommodation to the time sense of the increasing Gentile population in the Christian community, supported by three important theological recollections:

❋ Jesus rose from the dead in the early hours of a Sunday morning.
❋ The Holy Spirit descended upon the apostles 50 days later on a Sunday.
❋ God began creating the world on the eve of the first Sunday.

"They told Paul not to go on to Jerusalem" (Acts 21:4). Paul returns to the Holy Land in stages, by sea and by land. The Ephesian elders weep, believing they will never see him again (Acts 20:38). The Christians at Tyre tell Paul "through the Spirit" not to go to Jerusalem (Acts 21:4). The household of Deacon Philip, and Luke himself, weep and beg Paul not to go (Acts 21:12–13). On other mission trips, Paul has been a paragon of flexibility, adjusting his plans according to his reading of the signs and the promptings of the Spirit. Now, however, firm of purpose, he continues traveling towards the holy city, "For I am ready not only to be imprisoned but even to die at Jerusalem for the name of the Lord Jesus" (Acts 21:13). Paul has no illusions about what the future could bring.

The danger is not just personal. Clearly, the condition of the church in Jerusalem is lamentable, and hardly any Christian pilgrims are going there any more. James is still there (Acts 21:18), bravely facing the clear danger, which in fact will claim his life within a few short years. James assigns bodyguards and suggests that Paul go through ritual purification to demonstrate his faithfulness to Jewish ways, but in spite of this, Paul is recognized, seized, and beaten. The tribune intervenes to save him, is surprised when Paul speaks in Greek, and then lets him address the people.

"He addressed them in the Hebrew language" (Acts 22:2). On trial as a notorious Hellenizer, Paul seizes the attention of the jury by speaking to them in Hebrew. During the First Century, Hebrew was no longer a native tongue among the Jews, but many studied to the point where they were fluent in it as a second language. To be able to give a public address in the national tongue was a great accomplishment, a sign of outstanding scholarship. Paul could discuss Greek philosophy on the agora of Athens (Acts 17:22–31), and could discuss Hebrew theology in the council of the Sanhedrin.

Language is not one of the lesser gifts. No one can preach the gospel without using language. Therefore, the Church Universal has had to learn every vernacular language. Alongside the use of ritual languages by the Jews and by the traditional rites of the Church, the message has always been proclaimed in the language of ordinary people. Paul combines in his one person this linguistic two-edged sword, because he spoke the ritual Hebrew in Jerusalem, but also the Koine Greek in Antioch and elsewhere.

Some of the members of the Sanhedrin do not know Hebrew as well as Paul does, and hardly any of them know Greek so well. Many of them are silenced by the fact that they do not have his linguistic skills. Just by addressing them in Hebrew, Paul has already neutralized a good section of the jury.

"Brethren, I am a Pharisee, a son of Pharisees" (Acts 23:6). Twenty-three years before, the young Pharisee Saul had his experience of the Lord Jesus on the road to Damascus, and from that time on his former enemies became his friends, and his former friends became his enemies. Nevertheless, the excellent rabbinic education that the Pharisee Saul received remained useful throughout the life of the Apostle Paul. Here at trial, he knows his enemy, because he belongs to them. He never renounced Judaism, never renounced his rabbinic education. Now he uses that knowledge to divide and conquer those presuming to place him on trial. The judges may have prejudged him as a Sadducee, but he surprises them all by aligning himself with the Pharisees.

The Sanhedrin was a large body with diverse membership, especially representatives from among both the Sadducees and Pharisees. They coexisted well enough, but their differences were pronounced. Sadducees accommodated themselves to Greco-Roman culture, while Pharisees were uncompromising. Influenced by Greek philosophy, Sadducees denied the existence of life after death, but Pharisees believed in the final resurrection of all humanity on the Last Day. Obviously, insofar as resurrection is concerned, Paul took only a short step from his original belief in a general resurrection to his subsequent belief in the particular Resurrection of Jesus of Nazareth. Athenians and Sadducees tripped over the thought of any kind of resurrection, but Pharisees needed to make one, big step to the miracle of Easter—the Resurrection of the crucified Jesus Christ from the dead, after having spent three days buried in a guarded tomb.

Paul takes advantage of this fundamental philosophical difference among his adversaries and sets them to fighting with each other. The result is a hung jury, an impasse, which makes it impossible for the magistrates to come to a conclusion about Paul's case. When Jesus met the same tribunal, he remained silent because he wanted us all to go to heaven, but Paul does not become silent, because before he goes to heaven he wants to go to Rome.

"I worship the God of our fathers, believing everything laid down by the law or written in the prophets" (Acts 24:14). Paul demonstrates true Christian apologetics as he defends his case before the Sanhedrin. He seeks common ground with his adversaries, trying to build on their shared values. Of course Christianity is not a rejection of the God of Judaism, nor has Paul ceased to be a Jew when he became a Christian. Already in his correspondence he has explored the relationship between his Jewish heritage and his Christian calling, and found them not to be antithetical to each other. This strategy has already been seen in Athens, when he pointed out to the Athenians that they had an altar to a God Unknown, and that he came as a spokesman for the one true God they did not know (Acts 17:22–31).

Although controversy follows Paul everywhere, he never provokes it. Often the first reaction of his listeners is quite positive, and only when troublemakers arrive from a previous town does the mood sour on him. So too, here in Jerusalem, Jews from Asia recognized him and denounced him, when he was only worshipping as a devout Jew in the temple. Paul is not the patron saint of rough preaching; he treads bravely on dangerous ground but never insults anyone. He even apologizes for rebuking the high priest, whom he had not recognized, quoting the verse "You shall not speak evil of a ruler of your people" (Exodus 22:28). Paul always advised people in every circumstance to be respectful of their parents, spouses, children, masters, and slaves. He practiced what he preached, boldly stating truth but not using truth as a weapon to dominate others, seeking rather their liberation.

"You have appealed to Caesar, to Caesar you shall go" (Acts 25:12). Like the trial of Jesus, Paul's trial takes place before several tribunals. Both Jesus and Paul appear first before the religious tribunal, the Sanhedrin, because the charges against them are essentially religious in nature. The presiding judge for Jesus was the high priest Caiaphas; for Paul, the high priest Ananias (Acts 24:1). Although Mosaic Law prescribed a range of penalties up to and including the death penalty, the Romans had stripped the Jewish courts of the right to impose capital punishment. For this reason, both Jesus and Paul are sent over to the military court, in the person of the Roman commanding officer, the Prefect of Judea and Samaria, Pontius Pilate in the case of Jesus, Antonius Felix and then Porcius Festus in the case of Paul. In both cases, the civil court of the Herodian monarchs also comes informally into play. Pilate sends Jesus to Herod Antipas, while Festus allows Herod Agrippa II to visit Paul in prison. Herod Agrippa II arrives with his sister Bernice.

The House of Herod has caused the House of David great suffering down through the generations. Herod the Great killed the infants of Bethlehem in order to prevent the Messiah from growing up. Herod Antipas had concurred in the death of Jesus. Herod Agrippa I had beheaded the Apostle James, Son of Zebedee. Now, in the fourth generation, the Herodian family has become more humane. Herod Agrippa II, like his predecessors, is an ally of the Julio-Claudians ruling over Rome, but the Emperor Nero has been acting strangely lately (having his own mother murdered last year), and when Herod Agrippa hears that Paul will be going to the imperial court, he wants to know who Paul is and what he will have to say to the Emperor. In fact, the king would be perfectly happy if Paul were simply set free, but once Paul speaks the words "I appeal to Caesar," then in Roman law the case must be remitted to the higher tribunal.

"I stand now on trial for hope in the promise" (Acts 26:6). Paul tells the king and his sister the story of his conversion. Felix thinks any belief in Jesus' Resurrection is a sign of madness, but Paul reminds the Prefect that he is speaking freely to the king. Paul has the right as a citizen not only to appeal to the emperor but also to exercise freedom of speech in his own defense. Luke heard this statement in person, and the account at the end of Acts should be treated in every way as trustworthy as the other accounts, even the one written by Paul himself to the Galatians.

Paul practices what he preaches about treating those in authority with respect. He treats the king with dignity as a real person and not merely as a functionary holding an office: "King Agrippa, do you believe the prophets? I know that you believe" (Acts 26:27). Paul tries to evangelize even the king and his sister, and invites them to believe that the promises have already been fulfilled in Christ. Perhaps his words in coming years will continue to resonate in their hearts, and they will come to faith in Jesus. History will deal them a rough hand. Herod Agrippa is stripped of his kingdom, but not of his life, at the time of the Jewish Wars. Bernice is denied the hand of the Emperor Titus in marriage, because of her Jewish religion. In all, they might have proven the best of the Herodians had the times not denied them an opportunity to prove themselves.

All his [Paul's] energy was placed at the exclusive service of Jesus Christ and his Gospel. His [Paul's] existence would become that of an Apostle who wants to "become all things to all men" (1 Corinthians 9:22) without reserve.

From here we draw an important lesson: what counts is to place Jesus Christ at the center of our lives, so that our identity is marked essentially by the encounter, by communion with Christ and with his Word. In his light every other value is recovered and purified from possible dross. Another fundamental lesson offered by Paul is the universal breadth that characterizes his apostolate ... because God is the God of everyone.

Pope Benedict XVI,
General Audience (October 25, 2006)

For the Church, although dispersed throughout the whole world even to the ends of the earth, has received from the Apostles and from their disciples the faith in the one God, Father Almighty, the Creator of heaven and earth and sea and all that is in them; and in one Jesus Christ, the Son of God, who became flesh for our salvation; and in the Holy Spirit, who announced through the prophets the dispensations and the comings, and the birth from a Virgin, and the passion, and the resurrection from the dead, and the bodily ascension into heaven of the beloved Christ Jesus our Lord, and his coming from heaven in the glory of the Father to re-establish all things; and the raising up again of all flesh of all humanity, in order that to Jesus Christ our Lord and God and Savior and King, in accord with the approval of the invisible Father, every knee shall bend of those in heaven and on earth and under the earth, and that every tongue shall confess Him, and that He may make just judgment of them all; and that He may send the spiritual forces of wickedness, and the angels who transgressed and became apostates, and the impious, unjust, lawless and blasphemous among men, into everlasting fire; and that He may grant life, immortality, and surround with eternal glory the just and the holy, and those who have kept His commands and who have persevered in His love, either from their beginning or from their repentance.

Saint Irenaeus (140–202 AD) *Against Heresies*, 1, 10, 1

1. Describe the amazing events in the following passages.

1 Kings 17:17–24	
Mark 5:35–43	
Luke 7:11–17	
John 11:17–44	
Acts 9:36–42	
Acts 20:7–12	

2. On which day of the week did the early Church celebrate the Eucharist?

Acts 20:7	
CCC 1329	
CCC 1343	

3. What two things does Paul foretell in Acts 20:17–35?

Acts 20:25	
Acts 20:29–30	

4. How will the people be sustained in Paul's absence?

Acts 20:28	
Acts 20:31–32	
CCC 798	

5. How did the people respond to Paul? Acts 20:36–38

* Share a time when someone who had ministered specially to you was leaving.

6. Identify a common activity in the following passages.

Isaiah 20:2–6	
Jeremiah 13:1–11	
Ezekiel 4:1–17	
Acts 11:28	
Acts 21:10–12	

7. How many Jews accepted the Gospel of Christ? Acts 21:20–23, CCC 595

8. What can you learn about vows to the Lord?

Acts 21:23–25	
CCC 2102	

* Have you ever made a promise to God?   CCC 2101

9. Describe the drama in Acts 21:27–22:29.

10. What hope did Paul place before the Sanhedrin?

Acts 22:30–23:11	
CCC 993	

* What does hope in the Resurrection mean to you personally?

11. What plot was uncovered by which relative of Paul? Acts 23:12–22

12. How did the tribune handle Paul's crisis? Acts 23:22–35

13. Describe the events in Acts 24.

14. What can you learn about the Last Judgment? Acts 24:15, CCC 1038

15. What is involved in having a clear conscience?

Acts 24:16	
CCC 1794	
CCC 2471	

* Explain the difference in *following your conscience* and *doing what you want*.

16. What happened in Acts 25:1–12?

17. Describe the drama in Acts 25:13–27

18. What does Paul recount again in Acts 26?

19. Explain Acts 26:22–23 using CCC 601.

20. What is the response to Paul's speech? Acts 26:24–32

* Write a short outline to share what God has done in your life—your testimony.

Chapter 21

Letters from Prison
Colossians 1–4, Philemon

**He is the image of the invisible God, the first-born of all creation;
for in him all things were created, in heaven and on earth, visible and invisible,
whether thrones or dominions or principalities or authorities
—all things were created through him and for him.**
Colossians 1:15–16

Jesus foretold that his apostles would have to suffer imprisonment: "They will lay their hands on you and persecute you, delivering you up to the synagogues and prisons, and you will be brought before kings and governors for my name's sake. This will be a time for you to bear testimony" (Luke 21:12–13). The apostles bring a message of spiritual freedom to a world chained and bound to sin, but that enslaved world finds the message of freedom threatening.

Human justice is imperfect at best. Innocent people, falsely accused, sometimes find themselves on death row. People of high ideals occasionally find themselves jailed alongside ordinary criminals. The apostles, like Jesus, experienced arrest and imprisonment. Luke recounts the imprisonment of:
* John the Baptist in the fortress of Herod Antipas (Luke 3:20),
* Jesus in the house of Caiaphas (Luke 22:54),
* Peter on three occasions (Acts 4:3, 5:17ff, and 12:4),
* John in Jerusalem (Acts 4:3),
* Various apostles (Acts 5:18, 8:3, and 26:10),
* Silas and Paul in Philippi (Acts 16:23),
* Paul in Jerusalem (Acts 22), Caesarea (Acts 23), and Rome (Acts 27).

Strict prison routine in those days included harsh interrogation and torture. Paul mentions how he has served Christ: "with far greater labors, far more imprisonments, with countless beatings, and often near death. Five times I have received at the hands of the Jews the forty lashes less one. Three times I have been beaten with rods; once I was stoned" (2 Corinthians 11:23–25).

Not all confinements involved such abuse, however. In Caesarea and in Rome, Paul was subjected only to a type of house arrest, with a single soldier stationed to guard him and with visitors free to come and go. Paul could keep writing materials and a scribe with him in some of his confinements, and he could both receive and send correspondence. From prison, he wrote four canonical letters:
* Philippians,
* Ephesians,
* Colossians, with content similar to Ephesians,
* Philemon, with people also named in Colossians.

197

Philippians stands apart from the other letters, and may have been written any time over a span of at least ten years. The other three prison letters seem to come from the same period of captivity, in either Caesarea AD 58–60, or Rome AD 61–63. Many scholars favor the Rome years when Paul was clearly free to accept visitors. Caesarea recommends itself for another reason, because Jews traveled back and forth to the Holy Land far more often than to Rome. These frequent travelers could bear messages on a regular basis between Paul's prison in Caesarea and the communities in Asia Minor. Some of these travelers are known by name—Onesimus, who carried the letter to Philemon, and Tychicus, who carried the letters to the Ephesians and Colossians, possibly in the same pouch.

From the prison correspondence one learns that Paul was rarely alone during his confinements. Others were arrested with him, and he may have been allowed to keep servants or helpers. Prison rules in those days allowed family members or friends to stay in the cell to take care of sick or elderly prisoners. Since Paul had some kind of medical problem, the jailors may have allowed others to attend to him. One of his co-prisoners is Luke, "the beloved physician" (Colossians 4:14). In the letter to Kolosse, Paul names nine fellow prisoners, most of whom reappear in the letter to Philemon:
* Timothy (Colossians 1:1 and Philippians 1:1),
* Tychicus (Colossians 4:7 and Ephesians 6:21),
* Onesimus (Colossians 4:9 and Philemon 10),
* Aristarchus (Colossians 4:10 and Philemon 24),
* Mark (Colossians 4:10 and Philemon 24),
* Jesus called Justus (Colossians 4:11),
* Epaphras (Colossians 4:12 and Philemon 23),
* Luke (Colossians 4:14 and Philemon 24),
* Demas (Colossians 4:14 and Philemon 24).

"To the saints and faithful brethren in Christ at Colossae" (Colossians 1:2) — Kolosse (*Colossae* in Latin) in Asia Minor is a city that Paul apparently never visited. He had sent his co-worker Epaphras, a native Colossian, to evangelize the city for him. Afterwards, Paul was too busy in prison in Rome and in Spain to make a big detour to visit Kolosse. So this letter, along with Philemon, is unique in the Pauline corpus, being neither a letter written back to an already visited community, nor a letter written ahead to a city scheduled for a visit.

The name Kolosse comes from the Greek adjective meaning huge, very large, or gigantic. One of the seven wonders of the ancient world was the great Colossus of Rhodes, a huge statue that stood astride the entrance to the harbor of Rhodes. After the fire of Rome, Nero erected a huge colossus of himself, which was torn down after his death. On that very spot in Rome, the Flavian emperors built a huge amphitheater, which came to be known as the Coliseum. Prisoners from the Jewish War constructed the arena, which could be flooded to allow mock naval battles. Over the top of the Coliseum, a squadron of sailors minded a huge tarpaulin, which could be spread over the top of the arena like a tent. In that showplace, many generations of Christians were slain by gladiators or by fierce beasts, so that the place is now considered holy ground. The Pope still goes to the Coliseum every Good Friday to lead an outdoor Way of the Cross.

"He is the image of the invisible God" (Colossians 1:15). Many Pauline letters contain Christological hymns, some of which have been assumed into the Liturgy of the Hours as canticles during Evening Prayer. Many scholars speculate that these hymns were already in use among the Christians to whom Paul wrote. If so, then Paul himself may have taught those hymns to them while he (or in this case Epaphras) was among them, and then in the subsequent letter, he is merely reminding them of what they have already learned from him. The hymns do not become less Pauline for having already been part of the oral gospel; rather they are more Pauline. Paul sent Epaphras to Kolosse to teach them a very high Christology.

"Low Christology" emphasizes the humanity of Christ. "High Christology" emphasizes the divinity of Christ. To the Colossians, Paul writes that in Christ "all things were created, in heaven and on earth, visible and invisible, whether thrones or dominions or principalities or authorities—all things were created through him and for him. He is before all things, and in him all things hold together" (Colossians 1:16–17). Here Pauline thought rises to the level of Johannine theology: "In the beginning was the Word, and the Word was with God, and the Word was God. He was in the beginning with God; all things were made through him, and without him was not anything made that was made" (John 1:1–3). Clearly, the prison experience has not lowered Paul's Christology. Instead, by identifying himself with the self-emptying of Christ, Paul has come closer to an understanding of Christ's divine nature. With his body in the pit, Paul's mind soars to the heavens.

"In my flesh I complete what is lacking in Christ's afflictions for the sake of his body, that is, the church" (Colossians 1:24). The height of Christology does not obviate Paul's afflictions. After professing so beautifully the divine nature of Christ, Paul turns now to consider the human nature. As God, Christ is infinite; as Man, by definition, he is limited. Each and every human body is capable of only so much suffering before it is extinguished in death. Christ suffered for the sins of the whole world, but his broken body collapsed under that great weight—once, twice, and three times on the way to Calvary—and finally expired in his last breath. Saint Thomas Aquinas taught that one single drop of Christ's blood would have been sufficient to save the entire world, because of Whose Blood that was. In God's plan the Lord Jesus gave superabundantly of every drop of the blood of his Body, so that he could not be outdone in generosity. We can, however, like the many martyrs, unite our sufferings with those of Christ on the Cross. Paul indicates here that our affliction, which could never have saved the world on its own power, has salvific value, when united with Christ's Passion. If we become members of Christ, then Christ is the one who suffers when his members suffer. The hands and feet and side of Christ, members of his physical Body, bled for our salvation. Great saints and ordinary Christians alike have found meaning in suffering through uniting their sacrifices with the great sacrifice of Christ. The same Paul, who said that we are saved by faith, said that in our flesh we can help fill out the sufferings of Christ. We cannot divide Paul against Paul, and choose which Paul we want. We are saved by faith in Whom, after all? By faith in the Crucified One!

"Slaves, obey in everything" (Colossians 3:22). As in the Letter to the Ephesians, Paul shocks our modern sensibilities by seeming to endorse slavery, a sinful social structure. Remember that Paul did not invent slavery nor did he ever praise it. Liberation for everyone is part of his theology—freedom from sin and death—no less for slave masters than for slaves. Part of the reason Paul's words look so heartless is because our image of slavery comes from the cruel practices in the Old South. Slavery in ancient times was more humane in a number of respects. The Mosaic Law did not allow lifelong slavery—every seventh year slaves had to be set free; hence what the Old Testament meant by slavery was a seven-year period of indentured service. In the Greco-Roman world, educated people often worked as household slaves for the very rich, serving as their accountants and personal secretaries. Nonetheless, slavery was never an enviable condition, and skeletons of slaves have been identified in the volcanic mud of Herculaneum by the scarring where their tendons were stretched from heavy lifting. Paul's advice to slaves to obey "in singleness of heart" must be counterbalanced by his advice to slave owners to treat their slaves "justly and fairly, knowing that you also have a Master in heaven" (Colossians 4:1).

Think of why Paul meditates on slavery in his letters from prison. What do slaves and prisoners both have in common? They both lack freedom. Paul had been deprived of physical liberty and, in the depth of that experience, he found empathic faith. He has united his afflictions with those of Christ on the Cross, and he encourages slaves—and everyone else who suffers—to do the same thing. Paul identifies himself with the slaves, not the masters. Otherwise, he would not have been faithful to his Master, who came not to be served, but to serve.

"No longer as a slave but more than a slave" (Philemon 16). The topic of slavery resurfaces in one verse of the little Letter to Philemon. When Paul writes that letter, he has with him a fellow by the name of Onesimus, who has left Colossae but whom Paul is sending back. Some scholars say that Onesimus was a runaway slave, whom Paul converted to Christianity, and is returning to his slave owner Philemon, who is also a Christian. The word for slave in Greek can be translated either "slave" or "servant," so another possible translation of the verse is "no longer a servant but more than a servant." That translation would indicate that Paul has invested Onesimus with some kind of spiritual authority, as a deacon, or an elder, or a co-worker with Paul. That would be more easily reconciled with the other context where this man's name appears, "Onesimus, the faithful and beloved brother, who is one of yourselves" (Colossians 4:9). After his liberation or his ordination (which do not mutually exclude each other), Onesimus could be described in such a way, but not before. This would date the Letter to the Colossians a short while after the Letter to Philemon.

About forty years later, Ignatius of Antioch writes a letter to a Bishop of Ephesus, who bears the name Onesimus. If this is the same man, he must have been about twenty years old at the time Paul knew him, and about sixty years of age when Ignatius writes to him. That is not out of the realm of possibility. If true, that would indicate that a former slave rose to the position of bishop in the early church, and that the church took seriously the implications of its own theology of freedom.

Another modern speculation is that the Letters to Philemon and to the Ephesians, which are so unlike the other letters, were saved because the editor of the Pauline corpus was none other than Bishop Onesimus, the former slave. If so, then he lived up to his name, which means "useful," by proving himself useful not only to Paul, but also to the entire church. Somebody collected all of these letters, after all, and if it was not Onesimus, it was someone else who was very useful indeed.

During the time of his earthly pilgrimage, the disciple can already share through communion with the Son in his divine life and that of the Father: "our fellowship is with the Father and with his Son Jesus Christ" (1 John 1:3).

This life of fellowship with God and with one another is the proper goal of Gospel proclamation, the goal of conversion to Christianity: "That which we have seen and heard we proclaim also to you, so that you may have fellowship with us" (1 John 1:2). … Let us now go a step further. Communion, a fruit of the Holy Spirit, is nourished by the Eucharistic Bread (1 Corinthians 10:16–17) and is expressed in fraternal relations in a sort of anticipation of the future world.

In the Eucharist, Jesus nourishes us. He unites us with himself, with his Father, with the Holy Spirit, and with one another. This network of unity that embraces the world is an anticipation of the future world in our time. Precisely in this way, since it is an anticipation of the future world, communion is also a gift with very real consequences. It lifts us from our loneliness, from being closed in on ourselves, and makes us sharers in the love that unites us to God and to one another.

…Communion is truly the Good News, the remedy given to us by the Lord to fight the loneliness that threatens everyone today, the precious gift that makes us feel welcomed and beloved by God, in the unity of his People gathered in the name of the Trinity; it is the light that makes the Church shine forth like a beacon raised among the peoples. Thus, the church, despite all the human frailties that mark her historic profile, is revealed as a marvelous creation of love, brought into being to bring Christ close to every man and every woman who truly desires to meet him.

Pope Benedict XVI, *General Audience* (March 29, 2006)

1. What can you learn about prayer from Paul?

Colossians 1:1–5	
CCC 2632	
CCC 2636	

* What can you accomplish through prayer? How and when do you pray?

2. How is one delivered from the dominion of darkness?

Colossians 1:10–14	
CCC 1250	
CCC 517	
CCC 2839	

3. Identify a kind of prayer from these passages.

Colossians 1:15–20	
CCC 2641	

* Write a short prayer of praise to God in your own words.

4. Explain the concept of "redemptive suffering."

Colossians 1:24

CCC 307	
CCC 618	
CCC 1508	

5. Describe the mystery of man's union with God.

Colossians 1:25–29	
CCC 772	
CCC 773	

6. What warning does Paul give in Colossians 2:1–8?

7. What is Christ's role and what does He do for us?

Colossians 2:9–15	
CCC 794	
CCC 1694	

8. Identify a contemporary temptation found in Colossians 2:18.

9. Describe the positive instruction given in Colossians 3:1–4.

10. What advice is given in the following passages?

Colossians 3:5	
Colossians 3:8	
Colossians 3:9	
Colossians 3:12	
Colossians 3:13	
Colossians 3:15, 17	
Colossians 3:16	

* Which of the above is the most difficult for you to do? How can you improve?

11. What can you learn from these verses?

Colossians 3:14	
CCC 1827	
CCC 1844	

12. What order should be modeled in the Christian family?

Colossians 3:18	
Colossians 3:19	
Colossians 3:20	
Colossians 3:21	
CCC 2204	
CCC 2206	
CCC 2217	

13. What should slaves do? Colossians 3:22–25

14. Why should they be obedient? Colossians 3:24

15. How should masters behave?

Colossians 4:1	
CCC 1807	

16. What practical thing should every Christian do?

Colossians 4:2	
CCC 2629	
CCC 2638	

17. Paraphrase Colossians 4:6 in your own words. How can you really do this?

18. How does Paul greet Philemon? Philemon 1–7

19. What does Paul request of Philemon? Philemon 8–21

20. What does Paul ask in Philemon 22?

*Share a time when you offered hospitality, and a time when you received the same.

Chapter 22

To Rome and Beyond — AD 61
Acts 27–28

**And he expounded the matter to them from morning till evening,
testifying to the kingdom of God
and trying to trying to convince them about Jesus
both from the law of Moses and from the prophets.**
Acts 28:23

The written record draws to a close, but the story continues as the prisoner Paul begins his fourth missionary journey. Now, without mentioning his own name, Luke includes himself in the larger group of 276 persons aboard ship (Acts 27:37), as well as in the small group traveling with Paul. In letters from about this time, Paul refers to "Luke, my fellow worker" (Philemon 24) and "the beloved physician" (Colossians 4:14). As narrator, Luke participates in at least the second and fourth missionary journeys. Only an eyewitness could produce such a wealth of detail regarding the voyage to Rome. Luke and Paul celebrate the Day of Atonement together, for example, in Crete. Perhaps this is when Paul leaves Titus in charge of organizing the Cretan churches (Titus 1:5).

The Day of Atonement occurs in September or October, when the sailing conditions are becoming less favorable. Paul, already shipwrecked three times (2 Corinthians 11:25), advises against setting sail, but the sailors think they know better. So, off they sail into the tempest, driven off course to the south, then drifting for fourteen days. Finally, the sailors acquire some respect for Paul's seaworthiness, so they follow his advice not to leave the ship in the lifeboat (Acts 27:31).

In God's plan, the shipwreck allowed Paul to evangelize people on the island of Malta. After surviving the bite of a poisonous viper on shore and healing the father of the leading man, Publius, the prisoner Paul achieves hero status during his three-month-long stay on the island of Malta.

With the onset of fair weather, the prisoners and their guards catch passage on an Alexandrian ship called the Twin Brothers (*Dioskouroi* in Greek, *Castori* in Latin). Every port where Paul's ship stops will later take pride in being an apostolic church — Syracusa in Sicily, Regium (Reggio) in Calabria, Puteoli (Pozzuoli) near Naples. In Puteoli, Paul finds some Christians and stays with them for seven days before they accompany him up the Appian Way. The New Testament thus attests that Christianity reached the Bay of Naples area already by 60 AD. Twenty years later, when Mount Vesuvius erupts, Christians will be among those who lose their lives at Pompeii. In 1951, excavators discovered a cross on the wall above an altar in a second-story room of the House of the Bicentenary in Herculaneum, predating by centuries the earliest evidence of devotional crosses in Christian art.

"Paul was allowed to stay by himself" (Acts 28:16). With a soldier guarding him, Paul stays under house arrest in the Jewish quarter of Rome and receives visitors, including the Jewish elders. The Jews lived for the most part in the poorest parts of the city, especially across the Tiber River in the district called Trans Tiberim (Trastevere). There were seven communities, each with its own synagogue and council of elders presided over by a *gerusiarch*. Five Jewish cemeteries there have mostly Greek names and a few Latin ones, but with no Hebrew inscriptions.

In Acts, Luke says nothing about the Christians of Rome. Perhaps he did not want to slight anyone by leaving him out or endanger him by including his name. Paul mentions some of them in the last chapter of Romans. He was overjoyed to see his good friends Prisca and Aquila again, with whom he had stayed in Corinth and whom he had saluted before anyone else in the letter (Romans 16:3). Paul also meets the deaconess Phoebe, whom he sent to Rome bearing the letter (Romans 16:1). He also greeted twenty people with Greek names, three people with Latin names (Urbanus, Rufus, and Neuerus), and just one person with a Hebrew name, Mary. These proportions closely match the names in Rome's Jewish cemeteries.

The Martyrdom of James — In January AD 63, Porcius Festus, Prefect of Judea and Samaria, dies in office. During the three-months before his successor arrives, the religious authorities in Jerusalem begin to act with independence. A new high priest, Ananus, defies the long-standing restriction against imposing the death penalty, brings charges against James and some of his companions, and has them stoned to death. Two of the twelve apostles had the name James, a son of Zebedee and a son of Alphaeus. Back in AD 43, King Herod Agrippa beheaded James the son of Zebedee (Acts 12:1–2). Nineteen years later, the other James, son of Alphaeus, is martyred.

"Festus was now dead, and Albinus was but upon the road; so (Ananus the High Priest) assembled the Sanhedrin of judges, and brought before them the brother of Jesus who was called the Christ, whose name was James, and some of his companions. And when he had formed an accusation against them as breakers of the law, he delivered them to be stoned; but as for those who seemed the most equitable of the citizens, and such as were the most uneasy at the breach of the laws, they disliked what was done; they also sent to the king [Agrippa], desiring him to send to Ananus that he should act so no more, for that what he had already done was not to be justified: nay, some of them went also to meet Albinus, as he was upon his journey from Alexandria, and informed him that it was not lawful for Ananus to assemble a Sanhedrin without his consent. Whereupon Albinus complied with what they said, and wrote in anger to Ananus and threatened that he would bring him to punishment for what he had done; on which king Agrippa took the high priesthood from him, when he had ruled but three months, and made Jesus the son of Damneus high priest."

Josephus, *Antiquities of the Jews*, 20:9.1

Notice that Josephus testifies to the fact that some of the companions of James endured martyrdom along with him. This lends historical weight to the tradition that commemorates the martyrdom of the apostle Philip on the same date as that of James. For thirty-four years, longer than the Lord Jesus had lived upon the earth, the apostles Philip and James discharged their duties as apostles. James, called the first bishop of Jerusalem, steered the principal church community in the whole world, to which Jews and God-fearers came every Spring on pilgrimage.

Before long, word reaches Paul and Luke in Rome, and one can only imagine Paul's feelings at the martyrdom of his old foil, James. One need not imagine how Luke reacted—the evidence lies before us on the pages of his Gospel and the Acts of the Apostles. Word also reaches Matthew in Antioch, and he gets busy collecting the sayings and stories of Jesus. When he transcribes his list of the twelve apostles, Matthew (elsewhere called Levi, son of Alphaeus) places himself right next to James, son of Alphaeus (Matthew 10:3, Acts 1:13). Could they be blood brothers?

Liberation of Paul — In the year 63, the twenty-six year old Josephus went to Rome on a mission to intercede for some priests of his acquaintance, "whom on a small and trifling occasion" the Prefect Felix had bound and sent to the emperor for judgment. In his autobiography, Josephus writes:

> And when I had thus ... come to Dieearchia, which the Italians call Puteoli, I became acquainted with Aliturius, an actor of plays, and much beloved by Nero, but a Jew by birth; and through his interest became known to Poppea, Caesar's wife, and took care, as soon as possible, to entreat her to procure that the priests might be set at liberty. And when, besides this favor, I had obtained many presents from Poppea, I returned home again.
>
> Josephus, *Autobiography of Flavius Josephus*, no.4.

Although Paul was not of the priestly line, some of his companions were, notably Barnabas (Acts 4:36), and Luke mentions that many priests were among those who accepted Christianity (Acts 6:7). Two or more of those detained with Paul may have been priests known to Josephus, and thus Paul's release from prison could have been a result of the intercession of the Empress Poppea, who was Jewish (Josephus, *Antiquities* 20:8.11; Tacitus, *Annals* 16:6).

Paul in Spain — Tradition holds that after his release, Paul went on a missionary journey to Spain. Twice he told the Romans of his intention to do so: "I hope to see you in passing as I go to Spain" (Romans 15:24), and "I shall go on by way of you to Spain" (Romans 15:28). Upon landing at Tarraco (modern Tarragona), one of the first things Paul sees is the prominently positioned governor's palace, where Pontius Pilate was born and raised. Again Paul has reason to ponder the drama of the Passion, played out against the whole Mediterranean world, "from the rising of the sun to its setting" (Psalm 113:3). Paul thinks that the sun (Christ) rises in the east (Jerusalem) and sets in the west (Spain).

While Paul is most likely still in Spain, on the 19th of July in the year of 64, the Great Fire of Nero breaks out in the Circus Maximus and destroys eleven of the fourteen wards of the city. The poor quarter across the Tiber is spared, and the Jews and Christians who live there come under suspicion of arson. Christianity is not yet a banned religion, but the Emperor Nero collectively charges the Roman Christians of a plot to destroy the city (Tacticus, *Annals* 15.44). Both Peter and Paul are in the city when the first great persecution breaks out on June 29, AD 67.

Baptism in Blood — The New Testament does not describe the martyrdoms of Peter and Paul, along with many others. The Holy Spirit does not need to tell the readers of Acts that they are giving their lives for Christ; they know that already. Instead, the Spirit reminds the reader then and now, how salvation came through the passion and Resurrection of Christ, and how the faith traveled from Jerusalem to Rome by the great efforts of Peter and Paul and many courageous evangelists.

The Jewish War broke out in the Holy Land about the same time that the first Christian persecution took place. Thus, the powers of this world set out to dismantle the multi-faceted and rich Jewish life of the First Century. So many Jewish movements disappeared from history—the Sadducees, the Essenes, the Zealots, the Baptizers, and others unknown to us. Two movements would survive the general destruction, however, and become two of the world's great religions. The Pharisee movement would become Rabbinic Judaism, and the Messianic movement would become Christianity. While the world did the worst, God ensured that His people would endure and thrive.

Luke wrote formal introductions to both his Gospel and Acts of the Apostles. He put a nice ribbon on the end of his Gospel, so it is surprising how abruptly the Acts of the Apostles ends. Perhaps the Holy Spirit means to leave the work open-ended, so that there will be room for all of us in the continuing story. Guided by the successors of Peter and clinging firmly to the teachings of Paul, God's pilgrim people go onwards, bringing the message of the Kingdom of God to new corners of the globe and persevering into each new century.

God gives each generation a task that only they can do. Now, at the beginning of the Third Millennium, because of population growth, more people are alive than all the people who have ever died. That means that the church of our time is responsible for more than half the souls who have ever lived. At no time since the apostles has so much depended on the ministry of a single generation. If Saint Paul were with us now, he would be shouting out, "Behold, now is the acceptable time, behold, now is the day of salvation" (2 Corinthians 6:2). At this very moment he is interceding for the graces we need to meet our very great challenge. One of the ways God has answered his prayers is by giving us three great modern Popes named Paul—Paul VI (1963–1978), John Paul I (1978), and John Paul II (1978–2005)—who spent over forty years renewing the call to evangelize a world as much in need of liberation from sin as ever. Why should salvation belong only to generations past and not to people of the present and future as well? Where there is the culture of death, the guile of pride, the fixation of greed, the madness of lust, the blindness of despair, the pose of hypocrisy, or the fakery of legalism, the Spirit of God calls the people of the modern world to true freedom in Christ. Saint Paul and Saint Luke want us to know that, and to accept the great commission that Jesus gave to His apostles and to us: "Go therefore and make disciples of all nations, baptizing them in the name of the Father and of the Son and of the Holy Spirit, teaching them to observe all that I have commanded you; and lo, I am with you always, to the close of the age" (Matthew 28:19–20).

Let us go forward in hope! A new millennium is opening before the Church like a vast ocean upon which we shall venture, relying on the help of Christ. The Son of God who became incarnate two thousand years ago out of love for humanity, is at work even today: we need discerning eyes to see this and, above all, a generous heart to become the instruments of his work... The missionary mandate accompanies us into the Third Millennium and urges us to share the enthusiasm of the very first Christians: we can count on the power of the same Spirit who was poured out at Pentecost and who impels us still today to start out anew, sustained by hope "which does not disappoint" (Romans 5:5).

Pope John Paul II, *Novo Millennio Ineunte* (January 6, 2001) 58

The Church was built on the foundation of the Apostles as a community of faith, hope, and charity. Through the Apostles, we come to Jesus himself ... After Mary, a pure reflection of the light of Christ, it is from the Apostles, through their word and witness, that we receive the truth of Christ. Their mission is not isolated, however, but is situated within a mystery of communion that involves the entire People of God and is carried out in stages from the Old to the New Covenant ... So, from the first moment of his salvific activity, Jesus of Nazareth strives to gather together the People of God whom he came to bring together, purify and save.

... Thus, but differently from the Apostles, we too have a true, personal experience of the presence of the Risen Lord. Therefore, through the apostolic ministry it is Christ himself who reaches those who are called to the faith. The distance of the centuries is overcome, and the Risen One offers himself alive and active for our sake, in the Church and in the world today. This is our great joy. In the living river of Tradition, Christ is not two thousand years away but is really present among us and gives us the Truth, he gives us the light that makes us live and find the way towards the future.

Pope Benedict XVI, *General Audiences* (March 15, 2006 and May 3, 2006)

1. Why was Paul going to Italy? Acts 25:11–12

2. Describe the planned itinerary given in Acts 27:1–8.

3. Who was embarking upon this journey? Acts 27:1–3

4. Who is the writer of the Acts of the Apostles, who is with Paul? Acts 27:37

5. What can you learn about the evangelist Luke?

Colossians 4:14	
2 Timothy 4:11	
Philemon 24	

6. Describe the beginning of the voyage. Acts 27:3–8

7. What advice is given to whom, and how is it received? Acts 27:9–11

* Have you ever given or been given advice that was ignored? Explain here.

8. Explain some aspects of giving and receiving advice.

Proverbs 3:5–6	
Proverbs 13:1, 10	
Sirach 5:11–12	
Sirach 6:32–37	

* If you needed some good advice, to whom who you go?

9. Describe the drama in Acts 27:9–20.

10. Who brings counsel and advice to Paul?

Acts 27:23–24	
CCC 334	

11. Who is there to protect and shepherd you? CCC 336

* Do you pray to your guardian angel? Have you experienced protection and care?

12. What message does Paul share with the men? Acts 27:21–25

13. Explain the activities of the sailors. Acts 27:27–41

14. What was the soldiers' plan for the prisoners? Acts 27:42–44

15. Describe Paul's activity on the Island of Malta.

Acts 28:1–2	
Acts 28:3	
Acts 28:4	
Acts 28:5–6	
Acts 28:7–8	
Acts 28:9	
Acts 28:10	

* What gift would you give to someone who brought the gospel to you?

16. Describe the events in Acts 28:11–16.

17. About what or whom does Paul want to speak to the people?

Acts 28:20	
CCC 453	

18. How did people respond to Paul's preaching of the gospel? Acts 28:24

19. What can you learn from the following verses?

Isaiah 6:8–10	
Matthew 13:10–17	
John 12:36–43	
Acts 28:25–28	

20. What did Paul do in Acts 28:30–31?

* What practical thing can you do to advance the Kingdom of God here and now?

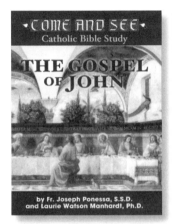

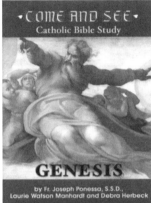

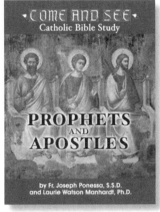

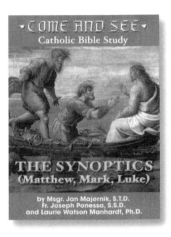

The Gospel of John

Provides a perfect starting point for Bible study. Twenty-one chapters reveal the theological understanding of Christ's life and the Catholic Church's scriptural basis for the Sacraments of Baptism, Reconciliation, Eucharist, Matrimony, and Holy Orders.
202 pages, $19.95

Genesis

Examines archeological and scientific facts to study the truths revealed in this Old Testament book. Twenty-two chapters present the beginning of human history and the lives of the patriarchs Abraham, Isaac, and Jacob.
206 pages, $19.95

Prophets and Apostles

Presents eleven Old Testament prophets looking to God's promised Messiah, while eleven New Testament books show the fulfillment of prophecy in the Passion, death, and Resurrection of our Lord.
206 pages, $19.95

The Synoptics

Takes you on a pilgrimage to the Holy Land and offers insights from biblical archeology, plus side-by-side comparisons of Gospel passages explaining the life of Jesus.
204 pages, $19.95

David and the Psalms

Studies the life of David and the psalms associated with his life. The twenty-two chapters begin with the study of Ruth, and continue with the study of David's life in 1 and 2 Samuel, concluding with the book of Psalms.
202 pages, $19.95

Moses and the Torah

Covers the Old Testament books of Exodus, Leviticus, Numbers, and Deuteronomy. Study the ways in which God reveals Himself to Moses, delivers His chosen people from slavery in Egypt, and gives the law.
220 pages, $19.95

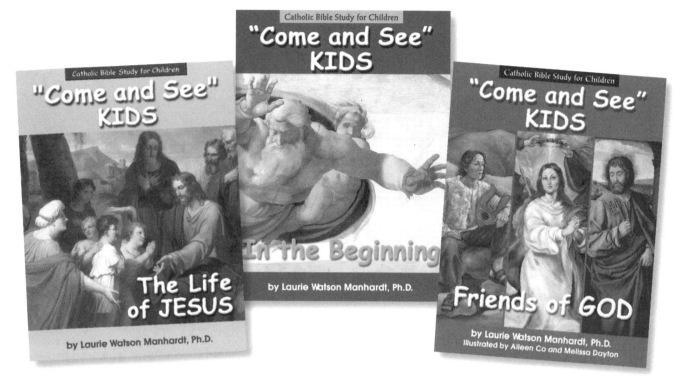